I love coffee!

I love coffee!

Over 100 Easy and Delicious Coffee Drinks

SUSAN ZIMMER

**Andrews McMeel
Publishing, LLC**
Kansas City

07 08 09 10 11 WKT 10 9 8 7 6 5 4 3

ISBN-13: 978-0-7407-6377-9
ISBN-10: 0-7407-6377-6

Zimmer, Susan
    I Love Coffee!: over 100 Easy and Delicious Coffee Drinks / Susan Zimmer.
        p. cm.
    ISBN-13: 978-0-7407-6377-9
    ISBN-10: 0-7407-6377-6
    1. Coffee. 2. Cookery (Coffee) I. Title.
TX817.C6Z56 2007
641.8'77—dc22

                                            2006049911

www.andrewsmcmeel.com
www.susanzimmer.com

This material was previously published in a different form as *Cappuccino Cocktails & Coffee Martinis: Specialty Coffee Recipes . . . and "A-Whole-Latte" More!*

Photos courtesy of: Ken Anderson: 93 (center), 109; Bialetti: 82, 8; Nick Brown: iv, xvi, 19, 52, 55, 56, 84, 86–89, 90, 121; DaVinci Gourmet Syrups: 95, 97, 104, 178, 191, 193, 198; Steve Ford: 93 (right), 116; Kerri Goodman-Small: 5, 7, 12; Kathy Ketner: ii, vi, 93 (left), 100, 123 (left and center), 124, 129, 143, 153, 163, 173, 177, 178 (left and right), 183, 187, 197; Liz Loop: front cover; Melitta: 36; Monin Gourmet Flavorings: 123, 148, 168; Oscar Einzig Photography: 174; P. F. Chang's China Bistro: 134; Dana Wilson: 60, 62, 64, 78–80; Susan Zimmer: 37
Food Stylist: Anne Fisher: cover, ii, vi, 93 (left), 100, 123 (left and center), 124, 129, 143, 153, 163, 173, 177, 178, (left and right), 183, 187, 197
Drink Stylist: Amanda Butler: ii, 183; Sammy Piccolo: front cover, iv, 84, 86-89, 121; Susan Zimmer: 174
Illustrations courtesy of Ingrid George: 34, 39, 41, 43, 45, 47

ATTENTION: SCHOOLS AND BUSINESSES
Andrews McMeel books are available at quantity discounts with bulk purchase for educational, business, or sales promotional use. For information, please write to: Special Sales Department, Andrews McMeel Publishing, LLC, 4520 Main Street, Kansas City, Missouri 64111.

In view of individual complexities and the specific natures of health problems, the author and publisher expressly disclaim any responsibility for any loss or risk, personal or otherwise, which is incurred, directly or indirectly, from the use and application of any of the contents of this book.

These recipes have been tested in U.S. standard measurements. Common metric measurements are given as a convenience for those who are more familiar with metric. These recipes have not been tested in metric.

TO MY FATHER, ALBERT ZIMMER, WHO TAUGHT ME:

Don't be fifty years old and wish you had done something you wanted to do when you were forty!

—ALBERT ZIMMER (1923–1978)

AND TO MY MOTHER, ROSE ZIMMER, WHO TAUGHT ME:

Where there is a will and passion, there's a way.

—ROSE ZIMMER (1922–2006)

Contents

Acknowledgments

My life has been my teacher and
I know life can be a grind, 'cause I've bean there!

MY BOOK'S ESPRESSO AND coffee recipes have been creatively designed, customized, and collected from various sources during my twenty-plus years in the coffee business—with the assistance of many and the inspiration of others. "Espresso thanks" to every individual involved in my journey, including my customers, coffee suppliers, and employers, for the knowledge, opportunities, and friendships I have gained.

Instead of claiming that I'm a coffee expert, I am very grateful for my überpassionate espresso enthusiasm and inquisitive curiosity for coffee information inherited over the last twenty years, which involves: family ties with my professionally trained "chef" relatives in Germany (who are always drinking *Kaffee*), and uncommon ties with people who have crossed my synchronistic coffee-life path.

There are others, closer to this book, by whom I feel blessed and to whom I extend a genuine heartfelt thank-you:

Bob (Bobbie) Morisset, my "spirit of significance," with whom I share my life. Without his stellar support, eternal optimism, and great patience, this project would have been much more difficult to complete.

My coffee-loving editor, Jean Z. Lucas (who actually went into labor with her first child at a Starbucks!), and her team at Andrews McMeel who have patiently and passionately worked with me in the evolution of this "cutting-edge" book.

I am expressly grateful to Albert Zuckerman, my literary agent at Writers House, in New York, and his assistant, Maya Rock, who both love coffee!

(Why, in the name of Juan Valdez, does one serendipitously encounter others who help one to better know oneself? Everyone I attracted along the way of conceiving and developing this book loved coffee! The coincidences I have experienced along my coffee-life journey have certainly been God's way of being anonymous, for which I'm truly grateful.)

My sincere appreciation to all of the manufacturers and companies credited in "Sources and Resources" for providing the recipe submissions and technical information needed to create this book. I also give great thanks to Maryann Oletic, Robin Jay, Amanda Stajan, Frank Roberts, and Sammy Piccolo; all the gals at Alberta Women Entrepreneurs; and many of my cherished customers and friends who deserve much credit for their being supportive and interconnected. I hope anyone, or any group, that has been overlooked will forgive me for the apparent perils to list one and all.

For more spiritual and synergistic awards, I thank my coffee-loving family: my father—now Guardian Angel—Albert Zimmer, who taught me at a very young age that in life we can have a "Taster's Choice" (that was his coffee of choice!); my mother, Rose Zimmer, who taught me "where there's a will, there's a way" and to also "never give up"; my only sister, Sonia, who taught me to "trust in all that is good"; and my Earth Angel children—my two daughters and my three stepchildren (our *Brady Bunch* family) and many precious grandchildren. I also extend a karmic thank-you to Susan Jean Zeloznicki, who is now my coffee-loving "Angel Publicist" in the sky. (I have this deep feeling that she is watching over me.)

Last but not least, thank you, coffee-loving reader—although apart, you are my friend whom I have not yet met. Cheers! I raise my cup also to those hopeless coffee romantics who were the first to sip steamed milk combined with espresso!

—Susan Zimmer-Morisset

Introduction

Let's Do Coffee . . . or an Espresso Martini!

*The conversation flowed between them warm
and refreshing, like a good cup of coffee.*

—ROSAMOND LEHMANN, *THE TIME OF LOVE*

DRINKING COFFEE AND, in particular, specialty coffees, has become a 2.25 billion-cup-per-day lifestyle. The world of coffee employs more than 25 million people around the world to sustain our coffee supply. Whether our beloved brew is purchased from a drive-through kiosk and consumed on the go, lingered over in a noisy deli, or sipped in a cloistered café, specialty coffee consumption has become a distinctive niche market in our society.

The emergence of the espresso era and cappuccino years have fueled this public phenomenon. Since our caffeine-craving taste buds and palates demand a higher standard of coffee quality and broader flavor varieties, passionate baristas and other coffee-making enthusiasts continue to serve up the best brews in neighborhood coffee shops or cappuccino pubs—our relaxing coffee comfort zones in today's buzzing society. This New Age beverage culture has penetrated many nontraditional venues, such as bookstores, supermarkets, gas stations, department and convenience stores, and airports. In some parts of the country, it seems a coffee bar has sprouted on every street corner!

Everything You Wanted to Know About Coffee and a Whole Latte More

Part 1 of this book is devoted to enhancing your knowledge about everything coffee. The first chapter, "The Wondrous World of Coffee," explores all the things you need to know about choosing, grinding, and storing your beans of choice. The second chapter, "Coffee Machines and Brewing Techniques," offers very important tips and information on how to make that perfect cup. A separate section devoted exclusively to espresso machines and espresso making follows in chapter 3.

Specialty coffee beverages have made huge strides in becoming part of most households, so it was only a matter of time before espresso machines would constitute the spiritual and aesthetic hearts of many North American kitchens. Home espresso and cappuccino machines have now become the kitchen roosters that greet a new morning for many espresso aficionados. If you love espresso and already own an espresso machine, that's a bonus. Certainly, professional and higher-quality espresso or cappuccino machines have become a popular purchase, enabling consumers to easily produce these coffee varieties in their own home. If you do not have one and desire to drink espresso—but your budget cannot accommodate an expensive machine—a basic stovetop espresso maker can be purchased for twenty to thirty dollars at most kitchen specialty retailers, department stores, hardware and housewares stores, or Italian delicatessens. More information about additional espresso makers is available in chapter 3.

New Kitchen-Café Buzz: Become Your Own at-Home Barista

There is no reason why you cannot perform your own ritual of brewing espresso and making cappuccinos in the comfort of your own "kitchen-café"—to entertain guests, nourish your soul, and please your palate (and maybe your pocketbook, too). The best news yet is that you do not necessarily need a special machine to make a creative coffee drink! The section "How to Make Basic Cappuccino or Latte Without a Machine" hopefully will inspire you to begin to brew and to create your own "coffee-teria" today.

The chapter "Making Coffee Drinks" will get into various tips for and methods of steaming and frothing milk for your favorite fancy coffees and the other creative coffee cocktails featured in this book. Once you're set with your choice of coffee beans and necessary brewing equipment, and have read the basic coffee-making and milk-frothing and -steaming tips, you can begin practicing your techniques like a real pro—a barista!

Also featured in "Making Coffee Drinks" is a special section, "How to Make Basic Latte Art," that illustrates some simple steps used by one of the world's top Barista Champions, Sammy Piccolo. We're also sharing some of Sammy's award-winning signature coffee drink recipes in part 2. Coffee enthusiasts who have mastered their personal coffee-making techniques and desire to take it up a notch will now be able to create visually exciting coffee art in the convenience of their own kitchens.

"Espresso-ism"—A New Age Coffee Recipe Renaissance

Loyal latte lappers and coffee-making observers that you are, many of you will wish to continue to return to your social coffee corners and stand witness to the talented baristas who practice their endless art of espresso expression. (That's why they are professionals—because of their endless repetitive "practice makes perfect!") This book will enable you to have a deeper understanding of their coffee creations, and of your own discernment between the many different kinds of coffee beverages.

Subconsciously, all coffee lovers play a supporting role in the drama of today's renaissance of coffee drinking. New coffee recipes are constantly being invented and distributed worldwide by leading coffee, syrup, and beverage companies, and baristas. New ranges of coffee drink flavors and recipes that coffee enthusiasts may never have considered compatible before are being revealed, expressed, and embraced.

I Love Coffee! reflects this abstract "Espresso-ism" we are experiencing. Our daily ritual to "drink in" or "take out" our favorite coffee leads some of us to develop a passionate thirst to learn more about the captivating brews we consume. Our continued caffeine cravings will perpetuate a demand for diversified coffee drinks and stimulate sippers from the potential coffee convert to the connoisseur.

Recipe Variety 101

Specialty coffee concoctions can be as myriad and varied as the blending combinations of coffee beans. Part 2 is devoted to more than one hundred easy-to-follow coffee drink recipes created and collected during my many years of coffee experience. Here, you will discover a wide variety of seasonally inspired beverages presented in five chapters. Sprinkled throughout are simple yet delicious recipes submitted by renowned coffee and syrup companies from around the world.

Please note that in these versatile recipes, espresso may be replaced by dark-roasted or strong coffee, whatever you perceive "strong" coffee to be. Espresso is an acquired taste; and often, if it is made improperly, it can impart a bitter taste. Like coffee, espresso has to be made with love and respect, to live up to its aromatic and flavorsome potential. The strength of the coffee, however, is a personal preference, so always be guided by your personal palate.

Also, nonalcoholic syrups may also be substituted for specified liqueurs to make nonalcoholic variations. A complete list of suitable syrups is itemized in the final chapter. Whipped creams, shaved chocolates, maraschino cherries, and coffee beans are just a few of the suggested garnishes for creating delicious coffee drink beverages that are easy and fun.

The Quintessential Espresso: A Martini Expressed

A special highlight of the recipe section is the chapter devoted to coffee and espresso martinis. During the early 1990s, we all watched with fascination as the conservative cup of coffee evolved into espressos and cappuccinos. Many thought that this espresso explosion was a trend that would come and go. Clearly, we have realized that these tantalizing drinks have become a permanent part of today's lifestyle. The unleashed possibilities of steaming and swirling captivating coffee concoctions have made their way into our hearts—and wallets!

Similarly, the traditional martini has evolved from its origins in the Great Depression through the debonair Rat Pack era to the wildly popular *Sex and the City* age. As with gourmet coffees, martinis have become a permanent classic beverage around the world. This American-invented cocktail is today being raised, held, admired, and reinvented . . . with shots of caffeine, creams, liqueurs, and syrups served in sleek and sophisticated martini glasses.

There's no question; a martini is a martini because of the glass in which it's served. Now—shaken, stirred, studded with coffee beans, and sweating caffeine—coffee and espresso martinis are quickly becoming the world's freshest coffee fashion drinks, in restaurants, lounges, bars, and household kitchen-cafés. Just when we thought cappuccinos and mochaccinos couldn't get sexier and sassier, the world's stage has raised the curtain on this new breed of cocktail-style coffee beverages.

In this aggressive and rapidly changing world, awareness and acceptance of coffee trends tend to transpire into a universal consciousness. Coffee and espresso martini drinks are of the "now" moment. The martini, just like the classic cup of coffee as we know it, will never be the same.

As already noted, please keep in mind that these coffee cocktails can be prepared either laced with liqueurs, or for nonalcoholic drinks, made with syrups instead.

Today's Trend—Tomorrow's Tradition

An endless variety of flavored syrups have always been a popular way to perk up sodas, infuse innovative flavors into "mocktails," and create decadent coffee drinks. Syrup manufacturers, beverage companies, and culinary drink mix masters worldwide are constantly using syrups and other flavorings to reinvent coffee recipes used in coffee shops, bars, and restaurants. This caffeination imagination is, however, "pushing the cup" in a re-birthing of a Generation X recipe renaissance, with the imminent arrival of cola-coffee recipe crossovers.

Passion and Coffee

Coffee, as a constant element on its own, interfaced with its use in infinite and creative recipes, has become a lifestyle perpetuated by passionate lovers of the bean.

Passion is the reason for everything we do, say, and feel. It's a state of mind and being. I believe, to get in touch with your passion, you have to somehow find the way back to your heart. I have loved coffee since I was very young, when I discovered decadent *Eiskaffee* (iced coffee) in my aunt Tante Maria's restaurant in Germany back in the mid-1960s. I patiently had to wait for thirty years before iced coffee started to become popular in North America, but it was worth the wait!

For some people, specialty and gourmet coffees are at the heart of life's simple indulgences. The coffee revolution has fueled our passions into a joie de vivre—a java joy within! In our society, which is naturally buzzing with overstimulation, it's ironic that coffee has the capacity to offer dolce far niente—the sweetness of doing nothing. It's as if people need to give themselves permission to relax and have a gourmet cup of "I'm worth it!"

Coffee drinking has always been associated with relaxing and sociability. So—if you love coffee—cocoon with your coffee cup, mug, or martini glass brimming with your beloved brew, and simply sip your way back to your center.

I Love Coffee! was written as a part of my passion and flow experience, to help serve you with an innovative and entertaining book about this vital beverage. My intention is to provide the ultimate guide for all coffee lovers. I hope that this book inspires you to follow *your* passion (open *your* mind, and obey *your* heart's counsel) to wherever life's daily grind may lead you. So . . . if you are ready to get perking, then grab your beans, read on, and let's get brewing.

PART I

Beans and Machines

Coffee beans and machines share certain common grounds—from crop to cup, there's a whole wide world of choices!

Chapter 1

The Wondrous World of Coffee

From America to Zanzibar, coffee is the drink that warms up the mornings of the world.

A CUP OF COFFEE, like any other experience, can be enriched by selection and conscious-ness. "No beans about it," the best coffee decisions are the ones most pleasant to one's own palate—the selection of one's coffee is a matter of personal preference.

Choosing coffee beans can also be a perplexing experience, because there is a huge range of coffee types and bean blends from all around the world. The final flavor and quality involves many complex factors, beginning with the coffee seed, the beans' botanics, a wide variety of soil and climate conditions, cultivation altitudes, and the care taken in harvesting the beans. Raw green coffee beans are then subjected to many influencing factors, including various processing, production, roasting, blending, and brewing methods. On a global note, the many species and varieties of coffee trees from different areas of the world also offer their own distinctive flavors.

There are more than forty-five coffee-exporting countries—all of which use different classification systems—that supply the world with coffee beans, in sizes ranging over sixty known species of coffee plants. No wonder coffee can involve a puzzling java jargon! Fortunately, the world's coffee nomenclature, from mountain to market, can be classified into simple categories.

This chapter briefly outlines the basics of bean botanics, coffee cultivation and processing, and global classifications used by the coffee trade and coffee-producing countries. There is a whole wide world of beans out there, and, theoretically, no amount of information can replace the actual art of tasting coffee, since "the truth is in the cup." However, the more we enrich our consciousness with coffee knowledge, the wiser our choices become, helping us to enjoy a better—not bitter—cup of coffee!

Explore now the wondrous world of coffee.

Coffee Bean Botanics—General Facts

- The coffee plant is a member of the Rubiacee family (genus *Coffea*), which grows in a narrow subtropical "coffee belt" that stretches around the world.
- Coffee plants are fruit-bearing shrubs that can grow from 10 to 34 feet (3 to 10 meters) tall. Cultivated plants are pruned down to 8 to 13 feet (2 to 4 meters) tall to make harvesting easier and to encourage broader, bushier growth.
- The plants first produce delicate clusters of white blossoms that exude a heavy, jasminelike fragrance. The very short flowering period varies from region to region. Small green coffee berries then appear and ripen to a bright red as they reach maturity. Within six to nine months, they turn almost black, ready to be harvested.
- The soft, yellow flesh of the berries contains two seeds, or "beans," each covered with a hard, protective covering. Inside that coating is a thin, pulpy, silvery membrane.
- The size of the beans differs in each of the sixty known species of coffee plants.
- The three best-known species of coffee grown commercially, each with its own varieties, are *C. arabica*, *C. robusta*, and *C. liberica*.
- The amount of caffeine in coffee beans varies by species. Robusta beans, which are responsible for the intensity and strength of the coffee, contain 2 to 4.5 percent caffeine; arabica beans, which are responsible for the aroma and body of the coffee, contain 1 to 1.7 percent caffeine.

Arabica Beans

- Arabica, the "aristocrats" of coffee beans, are grown at the highest altitudes. These are the most prized beans, demanding the highest prices in the world. They are the only beans used by the finest specialty coffee roasters and are responsible for brewed coffee's aroma, body, and smoothness.

- Arabica is the most widely cultivated coffee bean, constituting 75 percent of the world's coffee production.

- Arabica beans do best at altitudes of 3,000 to 6,500 feet (900 to 2,000 meters), where the slower growing process gives them a richer, more refined body flavor. The higher the altitude where the beans are grown, the finer the quality of the harvest will be.

- These beans need soil that is rich in minerals, and a constant temperature of about 68°F (20°C). They require very careful cultivation, with just the right climactic conditions, and are susceptible to disease, frost, and drought.

- Arabica shrubs yield 1 to 1¹/₂ pounds (500 to 700 g) of green coffee per shrub each year.

- Arabica coffee beans contain about 1 percent caffeine by weight.

Robusta Beans

- This coffee bean species is used for the lower grades of coffee sold throughout the world.

- This species does best at lower altitudes and elevations, even on plains, where the climate is unsuitable for the arabica species. It will do well even in poor growing conditions.

- *Coffea robusta* is very hardy and disease resistant.

- Robusta commands the lowest prices in the world, and its unremarkable flavor

and scent are undetectable when the beans are in lower-priced commercial coffee blends and soluble instant coffees. However, robusta is responsible for the strength and intensity of a finished cup of coffee.

- Robusta shrubs have a higher yield than do arabica, 2 to 3 pounds (1 to 1.5 kilos) of green coffee per shrub each year.
- Robusta coffee beans contain about 2 percent caffeine by weight.

Liberica Beans

- This coffee species is the third most recognized commercial variety and is similar to the robusta in that it also grows better at lower altitudes. It is hardy and can withstand poorer climate conditions.
- It is a minor crop from Africa.

These beans are my sole sustenance. They come from the berries on the hillsides.

—SHEIKH OMAR, TO THE CITIZENS OF MOCHA, YEMEN, A.D. 1258

Coffee-Producing Countries

Way down among Brazilians
Coffee beans grow by the billions
So they've got to find those extra cups to fill
They've got an awful lot of coffee in Brazil.

—FRANK SINATRA, "THE COFFEE SONG," LYRICS BY BOB HILLIARD, 1946

Coffee is second only to oil in terms of dollars traded worldwide. The world's green (unroasted) coffee trade is valued at $14 billion annually. Five geographic coffee-growing regions—South America, Central America, Asia, Africa, and the world's few coffee-producing islands (which include Hawaii and Jamaica)—are situated between the tropics of Cancer and Capricorn, where the climate is hot and humid. Within these regions lie the coffee-producing countries that supply the world annually with 91 million sacks, each weighing an average of 132 pounds (60 kilos):

- South and Central America produce 70 percent of the world's coffee supply.
- Asia and Africa produce 20 percent of the world's coffee supply.
- Coffee-producing islands (including Hawaii and Jamaica) account for the remaining production.

Of the worldwide coffee market, arabica beans account for 75 to 80 percent; robusta beans, for the remaining 20 to 25 percent. Following is a brief review of the world's three largest coffee-producing regions.

South and Central America

Ol' Blue Eyes wasn't just singing sweet Dixie when he estimated Brazil's beans to be in the billions! That nation is by far the world's leading coffee producer, supplying mainly high-quality, natural arabicas. Brazil is also the second-largest producer of robusta coffees, after

Indonesia. Brazil's Ipanema Agro Industria is the world's largest coffee-growing company. Their 12.4 million coffee trees, planted on 12,350 acres (123.5 hectares) of land, produce, on average, 15,000,000 pounds (6,810,000 kilos) of green coffee in a single good harvest year, nearly twice the supply of Jamaica and Hawaii combined.

Following Brazil, the next most prolific coffee producers are Colombia, Venezuela, Peru, and Ecuador, which supply washed arabicas (see page 10). Coffee production also plays a strategic role in the economy of Mexico, Panama, and the islands of the Caribbean. Their coffees, which are primarily washed arabicas, are generally very high quality as well.

Asia and Africa

India, New Guinea, and Indonesia have adopted modern growing methods over the years, thereby increasing their coffee supply of washed arabicas, as well as washed and natural robustas, which are marketed to the world.

Africa, located in the heart of the hottest tropical areas on earth, produces primarily robusta coffee beans. In the higher altitudes of Kenya and Tanzania, arabica coffee grows very well, yielding large quantities of washed beans.

Coffee-Producing Islands

"Other Island" is a catch-all coffee trade phrase that encompasses Hawaii, Jamaica, Puerto Rico, and the Galapagos Islands. Coffees grown in these regions are mostly mild, neutral without much acidity. These producers don't contribute quantum export quantities to world markets because they keep a majority of their crops, where they are sold profitably to tourist buyers.

Coffee Bean Cultivation and Processing

Coffee production requires a great deal of human effort, from the coffee crop to the last drop. Beginning with the prudent planting of the trees to the painstaking picking of the berries; from the washing, drying, and sizing to the sorting, grading, and selecting, the delicate beans rarely leave the touch of human hands. To value a cup of coffee is to respect the labor of love required—the caring human effort that was put into producing it.

Cultivation

- The most favorable seedbeds for the cultivation of coffee are soils that are volcanic in origin and rich in nitrogen.
- The optimum climate conditions are those prevailing in the tropics, where temperatures remain between 59° and 77°F (15° and 25°C). Wind, frost, leaf disease, and even excessive heat will destroy the shrubs.
- Plenty of rain, in combination with alternating dry periods, will produce the best crops.
- Carefully selected seeds are sown into suitable, prepared seedbeds.
- Slender shoots sprout up in eight weeks. After one year, the young plants are transplanted to permanent coffee plantation sites.
- Young plants do not bear fruit (berries) for the first two years; however, they still require great care in hoeing, weeding, pruning, and frequent watering to ensure proper growth.
- The plants begin their productive life span of 15 to 20 years after their first flowering that results in coffee berries and thus beans, with an annual yield of 1 to 2 pounds (500 to 900 g) of coffee per plant each year.
- When the coffee plant's delicate white flowers blossom, the orange and jasmine-like fragrance is as intoxicating as the flowers are beautiful; however, the blos-

soms are short-lived, lasting only two to three days. Clusters of green berries then appear, turning yellow, red, and then a deep crimson color. When the berries are almost black, they are ready to be harvested.

> Coffee farmers in Jamaica watch for bats, to judge when to begin harvesting their crop. When the bats start their nightly sucking on the sweet pulp of the berries, this signals to the farmers that it is time to begin!

Harvesting

The harvesting period varies from region to region, coffee tree to coffee tree, because not all of the berries ripen to maturity at the same time. The harvesting period may take several weeks and demand tremendous labor costs. There are two systems employed in harvesting—"picking" and "stripping."

- Picking ensures a perfectly uniform, top-quality harvest, as trained pickers expertly select only mature berries—one by one. Pickers of quality coffees must return to the same tree time after time, to pick more berries as they ripen.
- Stripping is used in some countries where plantations are vast and labor costs are high. This economical, labor-saving method is definitely faster; however, it results in a harvest of lesser-quality beans, since unripe and overripe berries are savagely plucked by machines along with the mature ones. A stripped harvest is usually rife with all sorts of impurities, such as leaves, stones, and unripe and rotten berries.

Once the berries are harvested, they are transported for the preparation and processing of the beans.

Preparation and Processing

To prepare the green coffee beans for market, they have to be removed from inside the berries that have been picked off the coffee shrubs. There are two methods of removing the two hard and pulpy outer layers: "wet" and "dry." In both methods, the seeds are sifted through meshes of various degrees of fineness and then graded and sorted by size.

THE "WET" METHOD

- This method is considered to produce a better bean. It is used for the hand-picked, quality beans.
- With this method, the coffee beans must be extracted from the freshly harvested berries within 24 hours. The berries are cleaned, the husk and pulp are removed, and then the seeds are steeped in fermentation tanks, washed, and finally dried.
- It is the fermentation stage that gives the beans a superior flavor.
- Sometimes coffees made from beans prepared by this method are referred to as "washed coffees," due to the beneficial soaking of the beans.

THE "DRY" METHOD

- This procedure is sometimes referred to as the "natural" method.
- The picked berries are spread in thin layers and dried in the sun or in heated dryers. Sometimes they are heaped together first, for a brief period of fermentation. Once the berries are dried, the pulp is then separated from the coffee seeds by a mechanical husker.

Sorting and Grading

The sorting of the beans can be performed by hand, machine, or a combination of both. However, humans with nimble hands are better able to remove unwanted materials such as stones, immature beans, twigs, and leaves. The more detail given to the cleaning and sorting process, the higher the quality of the finished beans—and the prices they can command.

The grading of the beans appoints value to various coffees for international trading. This sorting system is a device to control an agricultural commodity. Coffee-grading terminology is a language of its own, distinguishing one coffee-producing country from another, as pertains to certain bean criteria, such as:

- imperfections of the harvest, such as broken, immature beans or the presence of sticks, stones, leaves, etc.
- the size of the bean (the bigger the better)
- the age of the crop (how old the coffee shrubs are from which the beans were harvested)
- the altitude where the coffee crop was grown (the higher the better)
- the processing method used (wet or dry)
- the species (arabica, robusta, etc.) and then the specific variety of that species
- the plantation or area of production (this gives the region a signature market name)
- the cup quality (a criterion based simply on how good the brewed coffee tastes and smells)

After being graded, the green coffee beans are packed in standard 132–pound (60-kilogram) burlap coffee sacks, for shipment to roasters in consumer countries all over the world.

Coffee Roasting Chemistry

Nothing affects coffee flavor more than how the green, "raw" beans have been roasted. If you were to brew raw beans, the result would not possess any flavors recognizable as coffee. Roasting is the key stage, whereby the characteristic taste, aroma, and final flavor of the beans

is developed. The length of time of the roasting process also determines whether the coffee will end up being a "cinnamon," "city," "espresso," or "dark French roast." In simplified terms, coffee is described as "light," "medium," or "dark" roasted.

The Process

- In the roasting process, heat from an external source is applied to the raw coffee beans in large vats or drums, spinning and heating them evenly at temperatures reaching up to 550°F (290°C). The heat essentially creates chemical changes in the physical structure and composition of the beans.

- Water evaporates from the beans, starches convert to sugars, and the sugars caramelize. The beans increase in size by 25 to 35 percent. They begin to pop, much like popcorn. They lose 18 to 22 percent of their weight, mostly through this evaporation. The caffeine content, however, is not affected by these changes.

- Gradually, the green beans turn a yellowish color, then darken to a deep rich brown. During this color change, a number of chemical reactions occur, causing the beans' sugars and proteins to interact with each other. It is these changes, and the release of caffeol, or coffee oil, that are essential in bringing out the flavor and aroma of the beans. The darker the beans, the more oil they produce.

- Great care must be taken as the process nears completion, to ensure that the beans are not burnt.

- Flavorful acids form as the beans turn into a medium-dark roast. As the roasting progresses toward a darker roast, these same acids will now begin to break down, and the sugar components will start to caramelize. A darker roast has more body and an intense richer flavor to the palate. That is why espresso beans are characteristically low in acidity, rich in body, and sometimes caramel-like (caramel, after all, is just roasted sugar).

My Personal Favorite

The best espresso I have ever tasted was one that had been air-roasted. The beans were actually floating to roasting perfection upon a superheated, pressurized airstream within a roasting drum. The coffee beans never touch the scorching metal walls of the drum. In many roasting facilities, gravity pulls the coffee beans to the bottom of the roaster, where they can become burnt, blackened, or bitter. This burnt flavor is evident in the final brew. An excellent espresso should never be bitter. If it is, one of the reasons can be due to overroasting or poor roasting methods.

- After this monitored roasting process, the coffee beans are rapidly cooled down by jets of cold air, thereby sealing in all the flavor and aroma that the heated air has brought to life from the dormant green beans.
- The lighter the roast, the more flavor acids, resulting in interesting flavors and sparkle. Lighter roasts are lighter in body because the roast has not produced caramelized sugars or caffeol.
- Medium roasts have less acidic snap; they are richer, with a more rounded flavor. Here, coffee oils begin to appear.

- At the dark roast stage, all acidic tones disappear; the beans are oilier; there is a definite bittersweet, chocolatey flavor; the brew is rich and full in body and texture.
- An interesting note on roasting as it pertains to caffeine content: The darker the roast, the less caffeine content it will have. Higher, longer roasting temperatures eliminate more caffeine from the beans than will a brief, cooler roast.

Coffee Roasting Chart

The following classifications are used by professionals to designate the numerous darknesses of roasts:

Light	Medium	Medium Dark
Cinnamon	American	Full City
New England	Medium Brown	Vienna
Light	Brown	Velvet
Dark	**Darker**	**Very Dark**
Italian	Espresso	French
Espresso	Italian	Dark French
European	Continental	Italian

The Alternative: Roast Your Own at Home

All over the world, many coffee aficionados roast their own coffee, to enjoy the satisfaction of the ritual and the freshest cup of coffee possible. For those concerned about the environment, home roasting is ideal. A big sack of raw green coffee beans is certainly more economical than buying commercially roasted brands: home-roasting can curb the processing, packaging, and advertising expenses of purchasing small cans or bags of coffee at retail prices.

Nowadays, there are very good electric home-roasting machines, but for "back-to-basics" roasting, simply use a skillet on the stove top or in the oven. The physical procedures of these latter methods are also simple: first, the raw green coffee beans need to be kept moving in temperatures of at least 400°F (200°C) and, second, they have to be cooled down at the precise moment of the desired degree of roast.

THE SKILLET-ON-THE-STOVE METHOD

- ☕ Using an old, heavy metal skillet (with a handle and cover, and without a non-stick coating), spread only one layer of green coffee beans in the pan at a time. (An aluminum egg poacher pan works nicely.)

- ☕ Place an inexpensive oven thermometer in the pan. (Ideally, it should have a flat metal back that can be stood at an angle in the pan. It can then register the temperature of the air in the pan rather than the temperature of the bottom surface of the pan.)

- ☕ During the roasting process, smoke will start to seep out of the pan when the beans begin to pop, so make sure the windows are open, your smoke alarm is turned off, and the kitchen's air ventilator is on.

- ☕ Begin with medium heat and raise the heat until the thermometer registers 500°F (260°C). Then decrease the heat to a steady 400°F (200°C). Peek at the thermometer once in a while to be certain that 400°F (200°C) is being maintained.

- ☕ Holding down the cover on the pan, begin to gently shake the pan at 1-minute intervals, to roast the beans evenly. Anyone who has made stovetop popcorn will recognize this is the same technique.

- ☕ The beans will begin to snap, crackle, and pop! The beans will begin to change color, first becoming a yellowish brown, then swelling and darkening. Take a peek and watch the color, and stop roasting *just before* the desired color has been achieved (the beans will retain their heat and continue to darken for a moment or two longer).

- It is important to never let the beans darken to more than a chocolate brown color, or else they will taste burnt.
- Once the desired roasting has been reached, immediately remove the pan from the heat and dump the beans into another cool pan or onto slate or marble. The quick cool-down will close the bean pores to preserve the coffee's aroma, and halt the roasting process.

THE SKILLET-IN-THE-OVEN METHOD

- Preheat the oven to 500°F (260°C). Spread an even layer of green coffee beans (1/2 inch/1.3 cm) in an old cast-iron skillet and place in the preheated oven. Roast for 20 minutes.
- Shake the pan occasionally during the roasting time, for a mild to medium roast. The green beans will first turn yellow, then brown. The beans' natural moisture will begin to steam off.
- A "first crack" will be heard as the remaining moisture bursts from the beans and releases the coffee's rich aroma.
- For a darker roast, reduce the heat to 400°F (200°C) after 20 minutes, and continue to roast, stirring occasionally, for another 20 minutes (maximum) or less, depending on what degree of darkness you desire.
- Once the desired roasting has been achieved, remove the pan from the heat to cool the beans.

A NOTE ON USING STOVETOP POPCORN POPPERS

These neat stovetop pans can double as coffee roasters. Many kitchen boutiques sell them, retailing from $15 to $30. Follow the stovetop coffee-roasting directions. You will need to insert an oven thermometer to establish the proper temperature (as noted above) before the beans are shaken around in the pan.

"Cupping": Coffee Cup Testing

All of life is a dispute over taste and of tasting.

—FRIEDRICH NIETZSCHE (1844–1900), GERMAN PHILOSOPHER

Expert tasters are the aristocrats of the coffee industry. These coffee masters specialize in sampling small amounts of various coffee beans that are being considered for production and distribution. Professional coffee tasting is referred to as "cupping." It is similar to wine tasting, in that these experts can distinguish the very origin in a sample coffee blend, simply by smelling and tasting. There are, however, very few individuals who possess this rare ability. In fact, the New York Coffee and Sugar Exchange employs fewer than forty tasters that are responsible for all the coffee imported for the entire United States market.

Objective and scientific notes are kept, documenting the tasters' impressions of each coffee bean sample. The six standard criteria involve all five senses: Presentation, Sight, Aroma, Taste, Body, and Acidity.

Professional coffee tasters (known in the trade as "coffee cuppers") are passionate about their special abilities. They slurp the coffee violently and noisily from a testing spoon. The sample is almost inhaled, projected into the back of the mouth and sprayed on the roof of the palate, and is then rolled and almost chewed before it is professionally spit into a bucket!

This tasting exercise is certainly *not* part of my coffee-appreciating conduct! I tend to modestly smell and taste my coffee and then drink it down with grateful acknowledgment to the discerning gifts of the coffee aristocrats at the top of the industry lineup.

Coffee Blending Chemistry

The blending of coffees is an art. Each blend is the official signature of the inspired coffee roaster. Roasters, specialty coffee shops, office coffee services, and food-service companies usually offer their secret "house blends." Countless coffee creations are made worldwide by combining beans and roasts that complement one another with qualities the others lack.

The ability to balance the elements of the blend, so that no two types of coffees that are combined possess similar characteristics, is a principal skill for such artisans. For example, if both coffees are sharp and winey, such as an Ethiopian and a Kenyan, then these two would not marry well. On the other side of the cup, the most famous blend, Arabian Mocha and Java, offers ingredients with distinctive, extreme qualities, and together they produce a balanced rich, flavorful cup of coffee. The Arabian Mocha's mild acidity and light body couple well with the Java's heavy body and deep-toned flavors.

Recommendations for Blending Coffees

You can enrich any standard commercially produced coffee by adding the following:

For body and richness: Sumatran Mandheling, Celebes Kalossi, or Java

For sweetness: Venezuelan Maracaibo or Haitian

For even more sweetness, or to even out a bright, acidic coffee: Mysore

For a winey note: Ethiopian and Kenyan or Mocha for extra richness

For flavor and aroma: Kona, Sumatran, Celebes, Guatemalan, Colombian, or Jamaican Blue Mountain

For brightness, acidity, and snap: a good-quality Central American, such as Costa Rican or Guatemalan

Please note: The taste is up to you! Proportions depend on personal preference.

Flavored Coffee Beans

Flavoring coffee is as old as the beverage itself. The Arabs were the first coffee connoisseurs to add such spices as cinnamon to their beloved brew. Other Middle Easterners

followed, with the addition of cardamom, cloves, nutmeg, allspice, and even ground nuts. Spirits, chocolate, and citrus peels were also included later on. Once coffee was introduced to the Western world, the now-traditional cream and sugar were added to brewed coffee.

Flavored whole-bean coffees have made a fragrant appearance in specialty coffee shops and in local supermarkets' bulk coffee bins since the early 1980s. The variety of flavored coffees is amazing, the biggest sellers being French vanilla, Irish cream, hazelnut, macadamia nut, chocolate, and spice-based flavors.

Such coffees' assertive aromas come from the adding of artificial flavoring agents to the whole coffee bean during the roasting process. These chemicals sometimes leave a distinct chemical aftertaste. Some coffee manufacturers, however, use natural oils for making flavored coffee beans, extracting and using the essential extracts from a variety of flavor sources, such as vanilla and cocoa beans; cinnamon, cloves, and chicory; and various nuts and berries. These natural flavoring extracts are then compounded with other agents to produce flavoring oils that are used to coat the coffee beans.

Some flavored-coffee fans enjoy adding the flavorings themselves, in the way of syrups, to the beverage after it has been brewed. Italians have long been known for their variety of fountain syrups, and it was only a matter of time before these syrups found their way into coffee drinks. For more information on flavored syrups, see page 200.

Specialty vs. Commercial Coffee
Specialty Coffee

- "Specialty coffee" is the legal term used in the coffee trade for signature roasted coffees produced in smaller-scale facilities by private corporations.
- These are generally sold locally and possess a distinctive signature personality.
- Specialty coffees have inspired a common-ground culture for coffee connois-

seurs, and are a specialized niche, offering a wide variety of coffee choices with notable quality.

- Specialty coffee beans are usually well prepared, freshly roasted, and properly brewed.
- Specialty coffees offer superb sensuous qualities of aroma, flavor, and aesthetic satisfaction.

Commercial Coffee

- Commercial coffees are usually roasted, produced, and packed in enormous plants under nationally branded names, advertised ferociously, and distributed nationally and regionally.
- Commercial coffees are part of the organized retail food distribution network and are market-focused to sell to the mass consumer.
- Commercial coffees offer convenience and lower prices, but also present a very limited and often inferior selection of blends and roasts. They restrict the coffee connoisseur from experimenting with various coffee-blending creations.

Grinding and Storing Coffee

Oh, he could grind my coffee, 'cause he had a brand new grind.

—BESSIE SMITH (1894–1937), AMERICAN BLUES SINGER, FROM "EMPTY BED BLUES" BY J. C. JOHNSON, 1928

HERE'S A QUICK REFERENCE GUIDE TO COFFEE FRESHNESS:

Raw green coffee beans: retain their freshness for years

Roasted whole coffee beans: begin to lose their flavor after a week

Ground coffee: begins to lose its flavor within an hour after being ground

Brewed coffee: Begins to lose its flavor within minutes

Regardless of modern packing technologies, once a consumer opens a can or bag of ground coffee, the relatively fresh contents begin to lose aroma and freshness, due to oxidation. Oxygen, heat, and light are true curses to coffee, causing its delicate, aromatic coffee oils to deteriorate. Coffee also acts as a sponge, absorbing other scents. I can remember my mother placing a cup of ground coffee in the refrigerator to banish unpleasant odors. Also, it is suggested that one inhale the aroma of coffee beans to neutralize one's own perceptions of other fragrances, such as when sampling perfume.

The first way to maintain greater freshness is to purchase bulk coffee beans in small quantities and grind the beans just before brewing the coffee. Although this is not always possible, at least grinding your own beans can certainly offer a fresher cup of coffee than having your coffee preground at the store. Pregrinding is just a way of ensuring stale coffee. And this leads to the subject of grinds.

For optimal results, the ground coffee from a grinding machine must match both your brewing pot or machine and, of course, the particular variety of the coffee bean.

Tailor the Grind to Suit the Brewing Method

Different coffee-brewing methods require different types of coffee grinds, and different grinds require different lengths of brewing time.

A GENERAL BREWING GUIDE FOR VARIOUS GRINDS

Extra-fine grind—up to 30 seconds' brewing time
Fine grind—1 to 4 minutes' brewing time
Medium grind—4 to 6 minutes' brewing time
Coarse grind—6 to 8 minutes' brewing time

The shorter the brewing time, the finer the coffee grind must be, as when making an espresso. And, the finer the grind, the less you need. With a finer grind, more surface area of coffee is exposed for the water to infuse through it. This increased

COFFEE GRINDING GUIDE

This grinding guide is based on using an average propeller grinder with no more than four scoops ($^1/_4$ cup [125 ml]) at a time. Reduce the grinding time for quantities less than four scoops. Please keep in mind that both the machine and the person operating it can vary the results.

French Press

GRIND TYPE: medium to coarse (like bread crumbs); should feel like coarse sandpaper or cornmeal to the touch

GRINDING TIME: 10–15 seconds

Vacuum Pot

GRIND TYPE: medium, with little powder

GRINDING TIME: 15 seconds

Neapolitan Filter Pot

GRIND TYPE: medium to coarse, with no powder present

GRINDING TIME: 15 seconds

Filter Drip

GRIND TYPE: medium, with no powder present—just a touch finer than the metal filter drip grind

GRINDING TIME: 16 seconds

Stovetop Espresso (Moka) Pot

GRIND TYPE: medium to fine, like fine sand

GRINDING TIME: 20 seconds

Electric-pump Espresso Machine

GRIND TYPE: very fine. These machines require a fine, consistent grind with a texture between flour and table salt.

GRINDING TIME, WITH A HOME BURR MILL: 20–25 seconds

The Middle Eastern Method

GRIND TYPE: the finest of the finest, which should feel as soft as flannel, with the texture of flour.

GRINDING TIME: You may want to purchase this type of coffee in a specialty coffee shop or ethnic market, rather than attempting to make it yourself.

exposure of the grind's precious aromatic oils produces a more intense coffee. (In this case, less is more!)

Conversely, the longer the brewing time (such as when using the French press, or plunger pot, method), the coarser the grind must be. Coarser grinds require longer brewing cycles, where the ground coffee steeps in the water (as tea leaves do). If, for example, finely ground coffee is used for a plunger pot method, then the brewed coffee will be overextracted and bitter. Similarly, if a coarse grind is used to make a quickly brewed espresso, the coffee will be weak.

Grinders at a Glance

Grinding your coffee fresh from whole beans takes very little time, and it is inexpensive. It allows you to grind the beans in a way that accentuates what you like in a coffee, and what works best with your personal brewing method. Whether you use a sophisticated quickie electric method or a manual mortar and pestle, you will be releasing the rich oils that give coffee its flavor and aroma.

- Burr mill coffee grinders, similar to pepper mills, are popular in southern Europe and produce an important evenness to the grind for a more uniform brew. They are available in manual and electric models. The latter are great for quick and easy grinding. The cleanup is relatively easy, and some grinders offer an automatic timing device, good for lazy perfectionists.
- Blade-style electric coffee grinders use a small, electric motor to spin two metal blades at very high speeds, chopping and crushing the coffee beans. One disadvantage is that the blade grinder must repeatedly slice the bean, and this repeated contact can eventually heat the beans and damage their flavor. To prevent this, it is recommended that you grind the beans in short bursts of 3 to 5 seconds at a time, to keep the blades from "burning the beans" and produce a

more uniform grind. If you already use one of these to chop nuts or herbs, buy another—they are very inexpensive—to dedicate solely to coffee grinding, to avoid any transference of flavors.

- Box grinders—traditional Western coffee grinders—are often wooden boxes with a propeller blade that is turned manually. The beans are simply fed into a little door in the top of the box, and the ground coffee falls into a little bottom drawer as you whirr away. These are great, except for achieving fine grinds and for grinding larger quantities of coffee. Some metal models can be mounted on a wall or table; these can achieve a finer grind because you are not trying to hold the box still at the same time as you are grinding.

- A mortar and pestle is the most primitive approach to grinding coffee beans. This time-consuming technique is all done by hand and builds strong muscles, but unless you are a seasoned expert at using this tool, it will be difficult to achieve an even coffee grind. However, if you already love to make your own pesto or crush spices with a mortar and pestle, then this method may be the most aesthetically satisfying for you.

Why an Even Grind Is Important

The common and most important goal of every grinding method is to achieve an even, uniform grind, which will provide an even extraction of the oils from the coffee. Uneven, ill-proportioned grinds can taint the taste of even the finest of beans:

- Uneven coffee grinds will cause some of the coffee oils to overextract and some to underextract.
- Overextracted coffee tastes bitter and overly pungent.
- Underextracted coffee tastes weak, thin, and lifeless.

Storage Tips

Even after it has been roasted, coffee is a living organism, and, as it breathes oxygen, it releases carbon dioxide, which helps to preserve it. The trick to keeping it fresh is to prevent the coffee from being exposed to too much oxygen, while encouraging it to continue to produce carbon dioxide. Sometimes whole coffee beans can be purchased in "valve-lock bags" that do not allow oxygen to enter but allow the coffee's carbon dioxide to be released and held within the bag. As soon as you break the seal, however, you will need a proper container (as outlined below) in which to store the remaining coffee. Here are a few tips for storing coffee:

- Always store coffee away from its natural enemies: light, heat, oxygen, and humidity.
- Purchase coffee as whole beans and grind your own just before you use it so the coffee will stay fresher longer, as there is less surface area exposed to air and moisture during storage.
- If possible, purchase only a week's worth of coffee beans at a time. Store ground or whole coffee in an airtight, opaque canister (to prevent light from coming through).
- Ceramic or glass canisters with metal rings that latch shut are also ideal containers for coffee, since they cannot transfer any contaminants to the coffee.
- Never use a plastic or metal container. These substances produce a fair amount of flavor migration and penetration, which will corrupt the coffee.
- An odd tip, but it works: Cut a green garbage bag into squares, just large enough to line the inside of your coffee container. Store the coffee inside this bag, and seal the top of the green plastic with an elastic band. Keep this bag of beans or ground coffee inside the coffee storage container. The garbage bag material is ideal for preventing light, heat, and moisture from diminishing precious aromas and for preventing the coffee oils from going rancid. It adds extra protection inside the container.
- The storage container should be just big enough for the quantity of coffee to be stored, to prevent as little air (oxygen) at the top of the container as possible.

- Keep beans whole until you are ready to grind; then immediately brew the coffee.
- Only whole beans should be stored in the freezer, preferably in one-week's-worth packages.
- Never store coffee in the refrigerator, where it may absorb unpleasant odors and the temperature is not ideal.
- Ground coffee can also absorb freezer odors. Coffee oils, especially in darker-roasted beans, such as espresso, congeal when frozen, changing the consistency and harming the body of the brewed coffee.

For the Love of Decaf

Drinking decaf doesn't mean selling out on flavor, aroma or quality. . . . It should taste the same as caffeinated coffee if the caffeine is removed properly.

—ROSEMARY FURFARO, "DRINKING DECAFFEINATED COFFEES," WWW.SALLYS-PLACE.COM

Decaffeinated coffee appeals to certain coffee-lovers: those with sensitive stomachs, or who find regular coffee too stimulating, or whose sleep will be ruined by a caffeinated night-cap. To most dyed-in-the-wool caffeine drinkers, however, drinking the "unleaded" brew just doesn't have that same psychological kick as does the regular one.

The fact remains that even though the caffeine molecule, in its naked state, is a bitter alkaloid, caffeine loses its potency during the decaffeination and roasting processes. The hitch is, flavor and aroma compounds may also be diminished or removed during decaffeination. Although decaffeinated coffee beans are difficult to roast, it is usually the roasting process itself, if not done properly, that is responsible for the unpleasant tastes and textures of some decaf coffees. A superior decaffeination process, however, protects the original, rich flavor characteristics of the coffee when the caffeine is removed.

Based on my personal experience, a superior, 100 percent arabica, quality "air-roasted," Swiss water decaffeinated coffee can deliver a deliciously satisfying cup of decaf espresso or filtered coffee. I believe it could challenge any comparative taste test with a standard cup of caffeinated coffee.

The decaffeinated coffee market is achieving exponential growth. Today, it accounts for more than 20 percent of America's coffee consumption, as compared to only 3 percent back in 1962. Hence, greater demands for quality and variety go along with increased health concerns.

To make the best choices to suit personal preferences, you need to understand the various technological processes used by the coffee industry. The following general overview and information may help demystify decaffeination.

Decaffeination Processing Methods

A superior decaffeination process does for decaf coffee . . .
what virtual did for reality.

—SWISS WATER DECAFFEINATED COFFEE COMPANY, INC.

The process of decaffeinating coffee began at the turn of the last century, in Germany. Although there have been many patents since, today there are only three primary decaffeination methods used by the coffee industry. Each process begins the same way: the green (unroasted) coffee beans are moistened with steam and water to soften them, open their pores, and loosen their caffeine bonds. After this initial step, the following various methods are used. These methods are conventionally named according to the process.

THE SWISS WATER PROCESS, OR "WATER ONLY," METHOD

Swiss water decaffeination almost always uses high-quality arabica beans. Thus, the final higher-quality product is reflected in a more expensive price tag. Essentially, you get what you pay for.

This process does not use chemicals. First, the caffeine, as well as the flavor extracts, is stripped from the beans by the initial water and steam soak. This first batch of beans is discarded. The water, which now holds the coffee flavor extracts and caffeine, is filtered through carbon to remove the caffeine. Now only the "coffee-flavor-charged" extract (caffeine-free) solution remains. It is this extract that is used to subsequently absorb the caffeine from a *new* batch of beans. Due to the scientific principles of solubility, the caffeine in the new batch of coffee beans moves from an area of higher concentration (the bean itself) to an area of lower concentration (the extract). By this process, 94 to 96 percent of the caffeine is removed. Since this process uses no chemicals aside from the carbon filter (the same substance as is used to purify water), it is referred to as an organic, or natural, method.

THE WATER DECAFFEINATION METHOD

In a water decaffeination process that is not specifically "Swiss," sometimes chemicals, rather than charcoal filters, are used to extract the caffeine from the "coffee-flavor-charged" extract. It is important to note that this chemical solvent does not come into contact with the actual beans. The beans come into contact with water only, and the rich aroma and flavor characteristics of the coffee are minimally altered.

THE SOLVENT METHOD

Certain solvents, such as methylene chloride and common ethyl acetate, are the most widely used chemical compounds to decaffeinate coffee.

Although synthetic methylene chloride has been under fire as regards being hazardous to the environment, its use is allowed, providing the residues fall below certain limits.

Ethyl acetate may be sourced from natural ingredients, and it can be produced synthetically as well. This method is generally advertised as a "naturally" decaffeinated process. Unfortunately, there is no way of knowing whether the solvent source is natural or synthetic.

The Solvent-Touches-the-Bean Method

After the initial moistened phase, the solvent circulates through the beans, removing the caffeine. The beans are then rinsed with water and steamed once more, thereby easily evaporating any residual solvent, and finally dried. The beans are then sold to be roasted, and the extracted caffeine is sold for medicinal uses and soft drinks. This chemical caffeine method removes 96 to 98 percent of the caffeine.

The Solvent-Never-Touches-the-Bean Method

After the initial moistened phase, when the hot water bath has soaked the caffeine and the coffee extracts from the beans, the "flavor-charged" water is separated from the stripped beans and combined with a solvent, which unites with the caffeine. The solvent carrying the caffeine is then removed, and the flavor-charged caffeine-free water is reunited with the stripped coffee beans, to reabsorb the coffee flavors and oils.

It is important to note that when this method is used, the solvent never touches the bean itself. Again, any residual solvent is evaporated in the final steaming phase, or during the roasting process of the coffee bean.

The "Supercritical" Carbon Dioxide Method

Once again, after the initial moistening phase, the coffee beans that are being decaffeinated are put into an extractor. Pressurized "supercritical" carbon dioxide is used at 250 to 300 times its normal atmospheric pressure. At this pressure, the carbon dioxide turns somewhat into a fluid, having a form between a liquid and a gas. When this "supercritical" solvent passes through the coffee beans, the caffeine migrates to it.

The now-caffeine-rich solvent passes through a filter, to absorb the caffeine for reuse. When its work is done, and the pressure released, the solvent turns back into a gas and dissipates. Carbon dioxide is inexpensive to obtain and is nontoxic. This supercritical carbon dioxide method removes 96 to 98 percent of the caffeine without removing other coffee flavor characteristics.

Interestingly, whatever method they use, there are very few decaffeination processing plants in the world, because they are very, very expensive to operate. (This is also one reason why decaffeinated coffee is more expensive to purchase than regular coffee.)

Consumer Awareness: Ads for and the Labeling of Decaf Coffee

The majority of caffeine-free coffee sold in specialty stores is initially shipped to decaffeinating plants in Switzerland and Germany. It is in these countries that the majority of all decaffeinated coffees are produced. Once the processing is complete, they are then shipped back to North America. Decaffeinated coffee originated in Germany over one hundred years ago. It may be comforting to know that the processing standards are scrupulous and the quality controls of the decaffeination facilities are superior.

The U.S. Food and Drug Administration requires that coffee must have 97 percent of the caffeine removed from the untreated green beans to qualify as "decaffeinated."

When you are purchasing decaffeinated coffee, check to see if the decaf is an arabica or robusta blend. Depending on the type of bean and/or blend, the amount of caffeine that remains in the finished product can also vary. For example, the amount of caffeine in a decaffeinated 100 percent robusta coffee will be naturally higher than a 100 percent arabica coffee, since robusta beans have almost twice as much caffeine in their natural state as do arabica coffee beans.

Traditionally, inferior robusta beans are chosen for decaffeination because they yield a higher caffeine by-product, which is sold for medicinal and soft drink purposes. However, more and more arabica coffee beans are being decaffeinated, for their superior finished coffee flavor, aroma, and body, and certainly for the greatest benefit, a lower-caffeine coffee product!

Decaf Coffee or Mint Tea, Anyone?

Before you switch forever from decaf coffee to mint tea, concerned and careful consumers may be consoled to know the following facts:

- Methylene chloride evaporates at 180°F (83°C).
- Beans are roasted to at least 350°F (180°C).
- Coffee is brewed between 190° and 212°F (88° and 100°C).

Therefore, the amount of methylene chloride left in brewed decaf coffee is, in parts per billion, less than is in the air of many North American cities. Personally, I would be more concerned about fumes from a passing motorized vehicle before I would have any anguish over my cup of decaf!

Some General Cultural Coffee-Drinking Habits
- Italians drink their espresso with sugar.
- Germans and the Swiss drink coffee with equal parts hot chocolate.
- Mexicans, with cinnamon.
- Belgians, with chocolate.
- Ethiopians, with a pinch of salt.
- Moroccans, with peppercorns.
- Middle Easterners add cardamom and other spices to their coffee.
- Whipped cream (Schlag) is the favorite coffee addition in Austria, where it's customary to receive a glass of water with your coffee.
- Cubans drink coffee with milk in the morning and black with lots of sugar after lunch and dinner.

Chapter 2

Coffee Machines and Brewing Techniques

Making coffee in the French press versus the Neapolitan method is like French kissing instead of kissing on the cheek!

—ANONYMOUS

THERE ARE MANY WAYS to prepare a good cup of coffee. You'd be hard pressed (or perhaps French pressed!) to find a bad cup of joe these days. Whichever brewing style or tool is used, all methods have one thing in common: they all use hot water to extract the flavors and aromas from ground coffee beans.

Personal taste dictates the strength or weakness of the coffee, as well as the method with which to make it. Each method offers different advantages and disadvantages, achieves a distinguished coffee character, and attracts a different audience for reasons of culture, habit, taste, and/or lifestyle. Quality, convenience, simplicity, theatrics, or, perhaps, just plain passion also come into play. The following outlines the principal coffee-brewing machines and vessels to choose from. Please keep in mind, however, that besides the brewing method used, every finished coffee beverage will also differ greatly, based on the following factors:

- the kind of roasted coffee beans (see pages 11–14)
- the amount and fineness of the coffee grind (see pages 21–25)

Filter Drip Methods

Filter drip methods are the most widely used coffee-making techniques in North America and northern Europe. They permit the use of very fine coffee grinds for quick and thorough coffee extraction. Initially, a paper filter is placed in a plastic, glass, or ceramic holder. This filter holder sits on top of a flameproof glass carafe or coffeepot. Finely ground coffee is then placed in the filter. Boiling water is poured onto the ground coffee. The freshly brewed coffee then drips into the vessel below, while the grounds remain in the filter for easy disposal.

The Automatic Drip Method

RECOMMENDED COFFEE GRIND

Medium for paper filters; fine to medium for metal filters

THE METHOD

In an electric drip coffeemaker, place the ground coffee in a paper liner fitted inside the machine's cone-shaped or round filter. The hot water is heated automatically and drips through the coffee bed, trickling into a pot that sits on the machine's warming plate, known as "the burner."

BREWING TIPS

- To prevent a burnt flavor, never keep the coffeepot on its electric burner for longer than 20 minutes.
- Keep the coffee warm, if necessary, in an insulated thermal carafe. Be sure to first preheat the carafe with hot tap water, so the cold glass lining inside the carafe does not cool down the fresh hot coffee. Transfer the finished coffee to the carafe immediately after it has been brewed.

🫘 Blend the aromas of the finished coffee by swirling the coffee in the pot just prior to pouring the first cup.

ADVANTAGES

🫘 Set 'em and forget 'em! Automatic coffeemakers are ideal anytime you want a quick, convenient cup of coffee—especially first thing in the morning!

🫘 This is the best way to make coffee for a crowd.

🫘 Easy cleanup—the paper filters can be disposed of easily (if you compost, toss them into the mix).

🫘 A reusable wire mesh filter, often sold separately by the coffeemaker's manufacturer, may be used as an environmentally friendly alternative to disposable paper filters. A halfway measure would be to buy only unbleached paper filters.

DISADVANTAGES

🫘 Paper filters can absorb some of the coffee's flavor, and white paper filters have been processed with bleach.

🫘 A burnt, slightly bitter taste results when a pot of coffee remains on the machine's electrified burner too long (20 minutes or longer). Overheating it throws the finished flavor of the coffee out of balance.

🫘 Some coffee drinkers seeking to lead a more environmentally friendly life would prefer not to use electrical power to obtain their brew.

The Manual Drip Method

RECOMMENDED COFFEE GRIND

Medium for paper filters; fine to medium for metal filters

THE METHOD

Place the ground coffee in the paper or wire mesh filter that is designed to fit in a wedge-shaped filter holder
whose flat base sits upon a carafe or heat-resistant cup or
mug. Heat the water to boiling in a kettle. Allow the
boiled water to rest for 10 to 15 seconds, then pour it
slowly onto the ground coffee in the filter holder. The coffee will then drip into your container of choice. The best-
known brands of this device are Melitta and Chemex.

BREWING TIPS

- Be sure to preheat the container gently by rinsing it with hot (not boiling) tap water before filtering the coffee into it.
- Once the water has boiled, let it rest for 10 to 15 seconds before pouring it onto the ground coffee in the cone-shaped filter.
- Premoisten the ground coffee by initially pouring a little hot water over it, wetting it evenly. For example: If $^1/_2$ cup (125 ml) of ground coffee is used, dampen it with $^1/_2$ cup (125 ml) of hot water. Wait 30 seconds before pouring the remaining $2^1/_2$ cups (625 ml) of water through. The initial contact of water with the ground cof-fee releases a concentration of delicate coffee aromas and flavors. The premoist-ened ground coffee creates a smaller, denser volume packed into the deep bed, which enables the hot water to flow through them evenly.

ADVANTAGES

- Portion and waste control are benefits of this method, if only one to three cups are required.

- Complete control of coffee-to-water ratio and water temperature ensures a better-quality coffee than does the automatic drip method.
- The coffee flavors are not burnt or destroyed, as in the automatic method, where the coffee carafe is left sitting on a heated burner.
- This method is portable—great for camping!

DISADVANTAGES

- More time and attention is required for this method (however, a better quality of coffee is guaranteed), since one must boil water separately, then manually pour the water through the coffee in the filter.
- Careless pouring may result in a brew speckled with grounds.

The Cold-Press Method

This coffee-brewing technique creates a cold coffee concentrate. My sister, Sonia, introduced me to this method back in 1994. I'll never forget that cold-pressed and very passionate coffee experience—when she showed me her cold carafe "in process and purpose" in her fridge.

RECOMMENDED COFFEE GRIND

Medium

THE METHOD

The actual brewing container for this method is a big white plastic form fitted with a filter. The recommended cold-press coffee-making containers of choice are called the Toddy Method, and there is also one called the Filtron Coffee System.

Fill the brewing container with 1 pound of medium-ground coffee. Pour 4 cups of *cold* water over the coffee in the filter. Wait for 5 minutes—DO NOT STIR. Then slowly and evenly add 5 more cups of cold water. Again, DO NOT STIR. Place the container in the refrigerator. Allow 10 to 12 hours for the coffee to steep through the "Toddy," or cold-press filter. The liquid coffee will drain through the filter into a glass carafe. When the cold-filtering process has been completed, store the finished concentrate in the sealed glass decanter it has trickled into, and keep it tightly capped and refrigerated until use. This method yields 9 cups of cold coffee concentrate.

BREWING TIPS

- Hot Coffee: To microwave, add 1 part concentrate to 3 parts cold water, then heat. Or add 1 part concentrate to a container of kettle-boiled hot water.
- Cold/Iced Coffee: This is the premier method of making iced coffee because it blends so well. Add 1 part concentrate to 2 parts water, over ice. Cold coffee brewed this way makes great coffee ice cubes, too (page 131).

ADVANTAGES

- According to Toddy Coffee Makers, their cold brew system produces 67 percent less acid than does coffee made by conventional hot-water methods.
- Cold-brewed coffee is believed to have approximately 33 percent less caffeine than hot water methods. (As reported by MSNBC.)
- It's great for iced coffee recipes, coffeehouses, and iced drink–lovers. Add ice to the cold-press brew and you're done!
- This method is great for camping coffee. Simply add campfire-heated water to your coffee concentrate.

- The flavors of the cold-press method are weaker and less interesting to the French press and espresso enthusiasts (those techniques follow).
- If you normally make 1 cup to 3 cups of coffee at a time, the cold-press method may not be appropriate, as this method works best with a full pound of coffee, which produces more concentrate than you may desire to store in the fridge.

The French Press Method

The French press, or plunger-pot, method is easy to master and produces an extremely rich, robust coffee. It is the next best brew to espresso. The ground coffee directly infuses with slightly cooled boiling water, creating a promising marriage of flavor and aroma.

RECOMMENDED COFFEE GRIND

Medium to coarse

THE METHOD

Prewarm the glass beaker by rinsing it with hot water. Place the preferred amount of coffee in the beaker and fill with slightly cooled boiling water. Place the plunger lid on the beaker. The coffee should be allowed to steep for 4 to 6 minutes, then the meshed plunger lid should be pressed down gently through the coffee suspension. This separates the finished coffee from the grounds, which are pressed, or plunged, down to the bottom of the pot.

- Measure 2 level tablespoons (30 ml) of ground coffee for every 6 ounces (170 ml) of water.
- Water selection is also key. The higher the quality of the water used, the better your coffee will taste.
- Prerinse the glass plunger pot with hot (not boiling) water; add the slightly cooled (approximately 212°F [100°C]) kettle-boiled water to the ground coffee, then wrap a terrycloth towel around the pot during steeping. This will keep the finished coffee hot longer.

ADVANTAGES

- This method guarantees the richest body of coffee (if done properly), except for espresso.
- The steeping time is less than that of drip methods. The pressure application is slight; the water is hotter; the ratio of coffee to water is higher.
- The ground coffee steeps in water just under the boiling point, with no further boiling or burning, preserving the dark, delightful coffee aroma and flavor without a trace of bitterness.
- The delicate aroma of the coffee oils are *not* removed by a paper filter.
- This method is quick and it is also portable.

BONUS ADVANTAGE

The plunger pot can double as a milk frother to make cappuccinos and lattes!

Heat a cup of milk (nonfat milk works best), or soy or rice milk, in a saucepan on the stove, or in a microwave. Do not overheat or scald the milk. It should be heated just until it is too hot to put your finger into it.

Pour the milk into a clean, rinsed plunger pot.

Pump the plunger (top part) up and down in the pot for several minutes, as if using a butter churn. The milk will expand in volume by three to four times, creating froth for cappuccinos and lattes.

DISADVANTAGES

- The coffee may be cooled down by the time it has finished steeping.
- If the coffee grind is too fine, there may be difficulty in pressing down the plunger lid because of increased surface tension.
- Fine coffee sediment will remain at the bottom of the cup if a medium to coarse grind is not used.
- Extra cleanup is required, as this kind of pot has no paper filter.

The Vacuum Pot Method

This is the most dramatic and a unique way of preparing an excellent, full-flavored cup of coffee. Two glass globes, one set into another, with a filter, are suspended over a heat source. The setup looks more like a magical kerosene lamp than it does a coffeepot. Its sophisticated and attractive appeal was fashionable around the First World War and then again during the sixties and seventies. However, vacuum pots have lost much of their popularity, mainly due to their finicky and peculiar method.

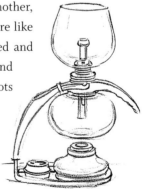

RECOMMENDED COFFEE GRIND

Medium to fine

THE METHOD

Place the pot's cloth filter in the upper funnel, and the ground coffee in the top glass globe. The coffee sits loosely around the filter, and the top is left open. Set the lower globe on its stand and fill it with boiling water from a kettle (if you wait for the small flame beneath the pot to boil the water, it will take hours). Fit the upper globe tightly upon the base, creating an airtight seal with the lower globe, and light the stand's low flame. Steam pressure will force the boiling water upward through the tube into the upper globe, where the water will begin to infuse the ground coffee. Stir the mixture, and allow the coffee to steep for 1 to 2 minutes, then turn off the flame. As the lower globe cools and contracts, a vacuum will form, and will suck the coffee down into the lower globe. When all the coffee has filtered down, remove the upper globe and pour the finished brew. Your guests will be impressed by your chemistry talents!

BREWING TIPS

- To help speed up this method, boil the water separately in a kettle, then pour it into the lower globe and light the vacuum pot's heat source to begin the steam-pressure process.
- Make certain the entire brewing process is complete before removing the top globe.

ADVANTAGES

- If you enjoy the theatrics of making an exotic brew, this method is impressive and entertaining.
- The pot is portable, and can be taken anywhere without any worry about electrical outlets.
- This method delivers an excellent, pure, fine coffee using a classic pot with cloth filters.

- This method is very time consuming. You definitely have to "go with the flow" with this one, since steam pressure is the driving force.
- The coffee brewing process must be absolutely complete before the top globe is removed. Patience and timing are crucial because if the top is removed too soon, the coffee will spill all over.
- Plastic models produce a muddy-looking brown coffee.
- The vacuum pot is a finicky and complex device.

The Middle Eastern Method

Each Mideastern country has its own variations of this method, such as Turkish or Greek coffee; however, all the techniques are similar in that very finely ground coffee is boiled with water and perhaps also sugar. This method produces a very heavy bodied, somewhat syrupy brew.

RECOMMENDED COFFEE GRIND

Pulverized to a powder as fine as cake flour

THE METHOD

A coffeepot called an *ibrik* (Turkish) or *briki* (Greek) is used. This is a long-handled copper or brass pot with a wide base and narrow top.

For two servings: Place 2 heaping teaspoons (13 g) of powder-fine coffee in the pot along with $^1/_2$ cup (125 ml) water and 2 heaping teaspoons (13 g) of sugar. Bring to a boil. When the coffee foams, remove the pot from the heat source; let the froth subside; stir. Repeat this heating process twice to produce a thick, black, muddy brew. Then pour the coffee into two 2-ounce (60 ml) cups. The grounds should be allowed to settle before the coffee is carefully consumed.

BREWING TIPS

- Never fill the *ibrik* to more than half its capacity. The coffee foams lavishly and the pot must accommodate this expansion. Otherwise, it will spill over.
- When the coffee foams and is about to boil over, remove the pot from the stove and pour a bit of the foam into the serving cups.
- The traditional custom is to pour the coffee immediately to ensure that everyone receives equal amounts of foam and coffee grounds. Some people may prefer to have the grounds settle in the *ibrik* first, but this thick, sweet coffee has a tradition and taste all of its own, which requires serving the grounds along with the liquid coffee.
- For spiced variations, add cardamom seeds, cinnamon, nutmeg, or cloves to the pot while the coffee is boiling.
- In the Middle East, the usual proportion of sweetener is equal parts sugar and ground coffee; however, this can be increased or decreased to suit personal preferences.

ADVANTAGES

- Once the grounds have settled, this heavy coffee is surprisingly mild and sweet if enough sugar has been added to it.
- The brewing process may be impressive and entertaining for guests.

DISADVANTAGES

- Producing a thin head of brown foam on the surface of the coffee is authentic to Middle Eastern coffee methods. However, it is not always achieved by a novice, so it may require some practice.

- People unused to this method may find the presence of coffee grounds in their cup disturbing to their coffee-drinking enjoyment.
- This brewing method requires a special, fine grind that is not advisable to attempt at home. If the coffee has not been pulverized sufficiently, the method will fail.
- It may not be easy to find the correct coffee and pot locally, and may be costly to order over the Internet.

The Percolator Method

In my opinion, boiled coffee is spoiled coffee. However, percolator-brewed coffee was quite popular during the 1930s and '40s. In this method, boiling water is force-pumped upward through a tube into a basket of ground coffee, literally boiling the coffee. Such pots drive away the delicate coffee aromatics and produce an overextracted, bitter brew.

RECOMMENDED COFFEE GRIND

Medium to coarse

THE METHOD

Fill the percolator with cold water. Place the ground coffee in the filter basket and insert the basket into the percolator. Cover and either place on a lit stove burner or if it is electric, plug it in. The heated water will create a steam pressure that forces it up through the coffee basket. The water repeatedly circulates over the bed of ground coffee, six to eight times, as the pot makes its characteristic bubbling sound.

BREWING TIPS

● Use only coffee that has been coarsely ground.

ADVANTAGES

● Its comforting aroma evokes a nostalgic memory of the catchy morning coffee music from television serials of the '50s.

DISADVANTAGES

● The delicate coffee aromatics and oils are burnt off, and the coffee achieved with this method is offensively distasteful and overextracted.
● Although there are various percolator styles and models to choose from, all of them produce bitter, lukewarm coffee.
● Medical research reports have consistently associated percolated coffee with high cholesterol issues.

Tips for Making the Perfect Cup of Coffee

Perfection has one grave default: it is apt to be dull.

—W. SOMERSET MAUGHAM (1874–1965)

Perfection is purely a personal choice. No matter how good a person thinks a coffee is, your own palate is certainly "the best judge of the better java," as far as your own preferences go. Whether you are taking the coffee straight up or immersing it in a lofty lather of frothed milk, there are certain freshness fundamentals that will perk up (*not* percolate, heaven forbid!) your coffee and make it live up to its aromatic and flavorsome potential. Every ingredient should be the best, the freshest; and every technique should be performed properly to ensure a perfect beverage. Of course, the best coffee teacher is practice, practice, practice!

CLEAN EQUIPMENT

- If sediments remain in equipment after use, the odors can be absorbed, and the remaining coffee oils can turn rancid, which will take a serious toll on future brews.
- Baking soda mixed with warm water is a great cleaning agent for nonpaper filters, coffeemakers, carafes, and cups (a pastelike solution of this will safely scrub coffee stains from even your finest china).

FRESH WATER

- Try not to use tap water for coffeemaking. The dissolved base minerals in hard water can cause a damaging buildup of hardened mineral and calcium deposits that can clog the fine steam and water channels inside your equipment.
- Chlorine-free, filtered or distilled water is most preferable (even carbon-filtered tap water is better than plain tap water), as these are free of any flavor or unfavorable odor that might distort the taste of your coffee.
- If you get water from the tap, start with cold water, because it hasn't been sitting in the pipes or the boiler for a long time.
- Whether to use softened water is a personal choice. Some people do not mind it; others say the phosphates and other agents in soft water produce a soapy-tasting coffee.

PROPER GRIND AND BREWING TIME

- The correct grind and length of brewing (contact) time the coffee requires varies according to the brewing method (see page 23).

PROPER QUANTITIES

- A standard rule when using a fine coffee grind is 1 tablespoon (15 ml) ground coffee per 8-ounce (250 ml) cup of water. If a double-strength brew is preferred, use 1 rounded tablespoon (22 ml) per $^1/_2$ cup (4 ounces [125 ml]) of water.
- If using a coarser grind, for example, as many as 4 rounded tablespoons (88 ml) per $2^1/_2$ cups (20 ounces [625 ml]) of water may be used.
- The most important rule here is: follow your own taste. This is a very personal choice.

PROPER TEMPERATURE

- When you boil water separately in a kettle, it should come to a full, rolling boil (212°F [100°C] at sea level, slightly less at higher altitudes), not merely a simmer.
- The correct water temperature is 195° to 205°F (90° to 96°C) when the water is in contact with the ground coffee, and should be 185° to 190°F (85° to 88°C) when the coffee has finished brewing.
- When using an electrical device, a good reference is the wattage on the coffeemaker: the higher the wattage, the more powerful the heater, and the better the coffee should be. Preferably, the machine will rate over 1,000 watts; however, most home machines are around 850 watts.

Chapter 3

Espresso Brewing Techniques and Tips

Espresso is the dark karmic soul of coffee:
Its combinations limitless, its energy timeless,
Prepared with passion, pursued with purpose.

Espresso Is . . .

- Extreme coffee. The extraction of espresso is a precise art form, involving an interdependence of factors within the brewing method, including the blend, the roasting, the grind, the proper temperature, the specific pressure, and the timing.
- Where the perfection of any specialty espresso-based drink begins.
- The basis for works of art to those who desire to create such ephemeral masterpieces.
- A kind of coffee cuisine; a passionate way of experiencing coffee.
- The essence of coffee intensified, a deepened coffee consciousness.
- A demitasse of intensely rich coffee, made fresh upon request "expressly" for one person.
- *Poco ma buono* (small but good).
- More so—more aroma, more body, more taste.

- The aroma of small, affordable pleasure.
- A potion of enlightenment, where the self-discovery journey can begin—*sit, smell, sip, silence.*

Espresso Is *Not*...
- Pronounced "EX-presso"!
- A degree of darkness of a coffee roast.
- The degree of fineness of a coffee grind.
- A species of coffee bean, a kind of roast, or a specific blend of coffees.
- A country where coffee is grown.

Espresso: An Extreme Definition

A true espresso is produced when 1^1/$_2$ ounces (45 ml) of filtered water, at a temperature of 195°F (90°C), is forced through ^{1}/$_4$ to ^{1}/$_3$ ounce (7 to 9 g) of finely ground, quality, espresso-roasted beans, at approximately 132 pounds (60 kg) per square inch, at 9 atmospheres (132 pounds per square inch) of pressure, with the water in direct contact with the coffee for approximately 25 seconds.

A quality espresso, when consumed, should leave a pleasant, not bitter, aftertaste, lingering on the palate for approximately 10 minutes, curling into an almost nutty flavor.

Brewed espresso contains over six hundred chemical components: sugars, caffeine, proteins in solution, emulsion of coffee oils, colloids, and coffee particles in suspension with tiny gas bubbles.

It takes approximately forty-two coffee beans to make one average-size serving of espresso.

What Is Crema?

Crema Is . . .

- A promise of sweetness, rather than bitterness.
- The dark, golden "cream" floating enticingly on top of the finished espresso.
- A uniform cream floating on top of the espresso, free of any white or light brown patches.
- The stickiness on the porcelain sides of the espresso cup, even after the espresso is consumed.
- A thick suspension of microscopic coffee oils and millions of microscopic gas bubbles.
- A rich blanket that should *not* dissipate within the first minute of being made.
- Filled with a full rich aroma, hitting your nose when you break up the crema with your first sip.
- The nectar of the gods.

The crema that crowns the top of a finished espresso is formed when the emulsified coffee oils are released (due to the high pressure on the grounds) and come into contact with oxygen in the air above the cup.

Once an espresso is prepared, its floral aromas develop first, while others, including the heavier, more roasted aromas, take longer to emerge. It is at this point that the crema is essential. It forms a "lid" over the coffee and prevents the most volatile vapors and aromas from escaping. In its buoyant perfection and crowning glory, the crema floats on top of the espresso.

Crema Quality—the Sugar Test

This creamy foam can be tested for quality simply by sprinkling a spoonful of granulated sugar onto an unstirred crema. The perfect crema may retain and keep the sugar intact for 3 to 5 seconds! Then the sugar will sink through the crema, creating a cone-shaped hole.

In Arabic, crema is called a *wesh*, meaning "the face of the coffee." To serve it with no foam is to "lose face"!

Low-Tech Espresso Machines

Like espresso itself, espresso-brewing methods are in a class of their own. Whether the espresso is consumed as an unadorned, straight "shot"; all dressed up with satiny frothed milk; or added to mochaccinos, specific factors differentiate these processes from regular coffee-brewing methods.

High-tech, high-cost commercial espresso machines are capable of creating the necessary pressurized extraction to produce an espresso in its finest form. These monster machines usually achieve the aroma, body, and crema characteristics of a true espresso.

How does one reproduce this dark, delightful coffee at home? Making espresso doesn't have to be difficult. Today's technology offers espresso makers in a wide range of prices, working in different ways and achieving various results. Low-tech and high-tech models are offered in various price ranges. All of them exhibit the same pressure principles; however, they all work by different processes.

If your passionate palate is intrigued with technology, and your budget can afford it, then the more sophisticated espresso equipment may be for you. However, before you take out a second mortgage on your house, consider some of the low-tech, simplified solutions first. These, such as the Neapolitan filter pot, may only require a budget of $20 to $30. The less sophisticated but more economical brewing methods are reliable, and are ideal for milk-based specialty coffee beverages.

Inexpensively made espresso may not win first prize in a professional barista contest, but Italians and other Europeans have perfected these humble techniques over many decades. They are the next best thing to a "perfect" espresso. For instance, the moka-style stovetop pot is perhaps the most popular espresso apparatus. It is found in just about every Italian household, and is manufactured in at least four different sizes.

The Stovetop Espresso Method

The simple moka pot is a traditional household utensil that brews espresso on top of a stove. Having a world-famous hourglass shape, this espresso brewer produces $1^1/_2$ to 3 atmos-

pheres of pressure, not the ideal of 9; however, it is enough to deliver some of the extra texture, body, and emulsion that gives espresso flavor and richness. Many seasoned Italian espresso connoisseurs prefer this method to any of the sophisticated machines that today's technology offers.

RECOMMENDED COFFEE GRIND
Fine to medium

BREWING TIPS

- Don't use coffee that has been ground too finely.
- Use coffee that is specifically roasted and ground for espresso making. Ordinary filter-drip coffee blends will not work.
- Experiment with different espresso brands to find one you like. Different brands can change the flavor, aroma, and body of the finished espresso.
- Never clean a moka pot in the dishwasher, or use steel wool or abrasive cleaners to clean it. It is recommended to rinse with only water.
- Periodically check the rubber rings (washers) inside the filter's "waistband" and replace them if they are damaged or worn out.
- Do not press down on the ground coffee when placing it in the filter. Instead, mound the coffee high in a pyramid shape.
- Before screwing on the top chamber, wipe off the rim of the bottom chamber to ensure a tight (but not too tight) seal.
- Make certain that the pot is not placed over high heat, but rather over medium or just less than medium heat. Once the water begins to boil, the espresso brewing process is rapid, and the coffee could become overextracted and bitter if it overheats.

The Method

PHOTO 1: Stovetop espresso makers have two chambers with a filter between them. The bottom chamber (the boiler) is used to boil the water. The middle filter holds the ground coffee. The top chamber is the pitcher that the finished espresso brews into.

With the central filter removed, fill the bottom boiler with fresh, filtered water until it reaches the height of the safety valve (visible inside the boiler), without going past it.

PHOTO 2: Insert the filter in the boiler. Fill the filter with the ground coffee, without pressing it down, distributing the coffee uniformly upon the filter. Remove any excess coffee from the edge of the filter.

PHOTO 3: After securely screwing the pitcherlike upper chamber onto the bottom, place the entire coffee apparatus on the stove (or over a campfire!) over medium heat. The water in the bottom chamber will boil, steam, and travel vertically upward through the ground coffee. In about 3 minutes, the brewed espresso will begin to trickle into the top chamber of the pot. You will know this is happening because the liquid

will start to gurgle and emerge from the pitcher's spout. Remove the pot from the heat and allow it to rest for a few minutes. The espresso is ready when steam comes out of the spout.

PHOTO 4: This "coffee fountain" style of preparation results in a rich, intense, delicious cup of coffee. When the pitcher is ready, pour out the espresso and enjoy it either straight up or in other favorite specialty coffee recipes.

A cousin of the moka pot is another stovetop model that brews the espresso directly into the cup. Not only is it convenient and inexpensive, but it also prewarms the cup at the same time. It works similarly to the moka-style pot; however, the downside is that it permits you to brew only one or two cups at a time, rather than an entire pot.

Note: This espresso apparatus is found in at least four different sizes in every single kitchen in Italy. If you are lucky and crema does crown your home espresso brew, count it as an astral blessing! Most moka pots cannot obtain the required intense pressure necessary to extract the precious, foaming emulsion of oils and colloids from the heated grounds. Bialetti's Brikka System is the only stovetop coffeemaker that produces the perfect crema.

- Although the moka-pot method does not guarantee a "perfect" espresso, it certainly is capable of producing a reliable, rich, home-brewed espresso that when coupled with frothed milk (see the French press milk-frothing tips on page 40), offers a thrifty home-kitchen alternative for making cappuccinos, lattes, and mochaccinos.

> Believe it or not, a shot of espresso has about half the caffeine of a larger cup of drip coffee.

- It is economical, portable, and low-maintenance.
- It is very space-efficient, is convenient, produces consistent results, and is easy to keep clean.

DISADVANTAGES

- It cannot be washed in a dishwasher.
- Instant coffee, coffee powders, and flavor extracts cannot be used with this coffeemaker. There are "mini varieties" now available.

The Neapolitan Filter Brewer

Italians call this kind of pot a *Napolenata* (Neapolitan) or *macchinetta* ("little machine"), the French call it a *café filtre* (a term also used for ordinary coffee made by the drip method into an individual cup), and Americans may refer to it as a "flip-drip" coffeemaker. This pot is a bit theatrical in that it requires a manual flip to turn it upside down.

Medium to coarse for Italian-made pots; medium to fine for the American-made pots

THE METHOD

There are two separate cylindrical pots that stack, joined at a "waist." One has a spout. Cold water is placed in the other, spoutless pot, and ground coffee is secured in the filter chamber in the "waist" of the vessel. The spouted pot is turned upside down and fitted securely upon the other pot, spout downward. The entire device is placed on the stove over high heat, the pot containing the water closest to the heat source. When the water boils and steam comes out of the spout, the device is removed from the heat and flipped over. The hot water drips through the coffee into the empty, spouted bottom of the pot. Voilà!—fresh espresso.

BREWING TIPS

- Preheat the bottom pot with hot water before brewing.
- Let the boiled water rest in the bottom pot for 10 to 15 seconds before flipping the device.
- Do not overfill the filter with the ground coffee.

ADVANTAGES

- This method is fun, easy, and economical.
- This method produces a rich, strong coffee.

DISADVANTAGES

- Sediment usually remains in the finished brew.
- If the handles are not heatproof, the flipping is not fun.
- Coffee should be transferred to a thermal carafe if it is to be kept warm for a while.

High-Tech Espresso Machines

The first espresso machine was invented in Italy in 1903 by Luigi Bezzera. Because of the brewing speed, he called this process *espresso*, meaning "express," as in "quick"; and indeed, espresso soon became the quintessential coffeehouse beverage.

This section discusses machines that you may find confusing and perhaps problematic. However, practice does make perfect—espresso! If operated carefully, these sophisticated home espresso and cappuccino systems can come close to delivering a professional cup, like those from your corner café. The fundamental difference between these machines and stovetop devices is the increased amount of pressure applied to hot, not boiling, water to produce the precise extraction necessary to create the emulsion of coffee particles, oils, and colloids from the ground coffee.

Another difference is that when the process is automatic, the hot water and ground coffee cannot stay in contact too long. The extraction is extremely quick. Almost instantly, as the pressurized water saturates every grain of ground coffee, the hopeful golden espresso nectar begins to trickle into the cup. The undesirable chemicals in the coffee do not get extracted. The desirables, however—the aromas and pleasant flavors—remain in the finished brew. Since the coffee is ground seconds before it is brewed, every cup is fresh.

If your discriminating palate has bought into the theatrical mechanics of a more elaborate espresso machine, then the following profiles of the three basic systems may offer helpful information and tips. If you are searching for a method that best suits your needs and lifestyle, then reviewing these profiles may help you choose.

Rather than elaborate on the methods in each machine category, I recommend that you read and follow the instruction manual for the individual machine you have or are choosing, since each machine has different features and manufacturers offer different directions.

Pump Espresso Machines

These expensive electrical devices for making espresso are comparable to commercial machines. The machine's operator pilots the control switch to activate a pump that raises the heat in the boiler or heating coil. This creates an intense pressure that forces the water through the coffee bed, producing a quality espresso usually crowned with crema. These machine models usually have a valve for frothing and heating milk for milk-based specialty coffees. The home machines use a vibration pump rather than the rotary pump of the commercial versions.

RECOMMENDED COFFEE GRIND

Very fine; the grind has to be just right to produce the crema, and should have a texture between flour and table salt. Tip: The ground coffee should feel like fine sand, with a bit of abrasiveness to it when you rub the coffee between your fingers. It should NOT feel as fine or soft as cake flour.

BREWING TIPS

- If possible, use water from a filter pitcher, or nonmineral water, for best flavor. The worst enemy of these machines is the mineral deposits that are left by tap water.

- Before brewing any espresso, perform a "blind" brew (technically called ventilating the machine) by running water through the machine without adding any coffee. This heats up all the metal elements and prewarms the cups, too. A preheated machine is also a step closer to obtaining crema on the espresso.
- Prime the pump to freshen the water in the boiler. This will also flush out any air pockets.
- If only one cup is being made, throw out the first cup of brewed espresso. The second cup will always taste better. (Maybe that's how the name of the Second Cup coffee chain franchise was born!)
- Models that have heavy, solid metal filters, filter holders, and group heads retain the heat better than others that are more lightweight.
- It's recommended to position the machine near a sink, as it is messy to use and requires extensive cleanup.

ADVANTAGES

- This machine supplies the proper pressure to ensure a very good espresso.
- Models with a large-capacity, refillable water reservoir can produce a continuous supply of pressure, to make many espresso drinks without any interruption.
- This method achieves a relatively rapid brewing temperature.
- Higher-quality machines today are built like tanks—they are made of stainless steel and do not wear out.

DISADVANTAGES

- Some lower-quality systems are very noisy and are not space efficient.
- This kind of device is very sensitive to the size of the ground coffee being used, and will not produce the desired results if the grind is either not fine enough or too fine.

Piston Machines

Piston machines are appropriately named since the spring-loaded, or hand-operated (or shall we say, "bicep-operated"), piston is the main characteristic of these devices.

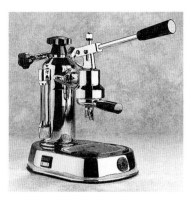

The piston does the job of the motor, the pump, and the brewing switches of the previous style machine— producing the same high pressure. In some regards, the machine works in the same way as an automatic drip coffeemaker. Cold water is poured into a chamber, and ground coffee is placed in a small container in the top of the machine. The piston is lifted, drawing up the water above the coffee compartment, where the water is heated electrically. A light indicates when the water is hot enough. Then the operator presses the piston down, forcing the heated water through the coffee bed.

This functional antique was very popular during the sixties, until the push-button pump moved into the piston's territory. Today, this device may be difficult to find; however, the piston machines are still regarded, by some professionals, as among the finest machines made, as they allow for closer, hands-on control in making espresso.

RECOMMENDED COFFEE GRIND

Fine

BREWING TIPS

- The size of the ground coffee is crucial to producing a quality espresso. If the grind is too coarse, the lever will go down almost effortlessly, since there is no resistance in the coffee bed, and only dirty water will be delivered into the cup. If the grind is too fine, you may have to overexert your biceps to push the lever down, as in this case there is too much resistance for the water to pass through the coffee bed.

- When the light indicates the machine is ready to brew, lift the lever almost immediately or it may be too difficult to push back down.
- Do not press the lever down too hard; just guide it down.

ADVANTAGES

- The machine looks very romantic and impressive, and makes for a great kitchen conversation piece.
- It produces a quality espresso (if used properly).
- It is simple in structure and design.
- This system is not as noisy as the pump machine.
- There is more control of the brewing pressure as relates to the coarseness of the coffee grind.
- This is a low-maintenance, reliable, durable machine; fewer parts, fewer malfunctions.
- Once the water heats up, the temperature (around 190°F [188°C]) is usually hotter than in stovetop devices and thus more ideal for espresso.
- If you don't produce a quality espresso, at least your biceps will have had a good workout!

DISADVANTAGES

- This process may be very labor intensive. The pressure applied is directly linked to the strength in your arm.
- If the operator does not apply enough pressure to the lever, the espresso will not be good.

- Conversely, if you press too hard, it will not be good either. Thus, the device offers very inconsistent results.
- This machine is not space efficient.
- It is time consuming—heating up the water reservoir for coffee-brewing (same reservoir for milk frothing) can take up to 15 minutes. The water reservoir in this machine cannot be refilled while in use. It must be allowed to cool down, refilled, and then heated up again.
- The water reservoir capacity is limited, as it serves both the coffee brewing and milk frothing.

Steam-Powered Machines

These electric espresso machines function like glorified stovetop pots. The biggest differences between the two are the price and the heat source. These overstated machines cost four to five times more than a simple moka pot, and are equipped with an electric heat source instead of necessitating the humble burner on the stove.

Sure, there is the bonus of the milk-steaming nozzle; which can sometimes be as useless as the disconnected hose of a fire hydrant. The pressure generated from the small boiler has only enough pressure to push hot water through the coffee bed. Any leftover steam pressure is usually insufficient to froth the milk properly, if you are planning to make specialty coffees. Many of these are simple aerating devices, which force the air from the room, along with the steam, into the milk. Unfortunately, the design of these machines is sleek and sexy, attracting consumers only to disappoint them with inadequate pressure, performance, and capabilities.

RECOMMENDED COFFEE GRIND

Medium to fine

BREWING TIPS

- 🫘 When using a model that offers an on/off switch to stop the flow of coffee, stop the brew cycle somewhere after the midpoint to prevent overextraction.

ADVANTAGES

- 🫘 A quick-fix method, this is a convenient way to make a mediocre espresso or caffe latte.
- 🫘 It is not sensitive to the grind of the coffee—anything goes with this machine.
- 🫘 It is capable of making several cups at a time—offering quantity if not quality.
- 🫘 The heat is provided by a built-in electrical element (no need to turn on the stove).
- 🫘 Models that have a switch to turn off the flow of coffee allow for overextraction control in the brewing process.
- 🫘 They also provide a means to divert the trapped pressure in the boiler to the next step of frothing the milk (if specialty coffees are being made).

DISADVANTAGES

- 🫘 Electric espresso machines fool people by their attractive designs, then disappoint by their incapability to supply enough pressure to create a true espresso. Most of the time they do not deliver any crema.
- 🫘 They are an expensive alternative to the more economical moka stovetop method. Essentially, the espresso results from the two are comparable.
- 🫘 The equipment attachments—the filter, filter holder and group head—are usually flimsy and lightweight, which does not ensure a tight seal.

- These machines are not space efficient.
- Generally, there is not enough pressure to steam a small pitcher of milk. Sometimes the purchase of a foaming gadget is necessary, or see tips on page 72.
- These machines are complicated to clean.

The Four M's: Musts for Making Perfect Espresso

Espresso is pleasure. . . . If it isn't perfect, where is the pleasure?

No matter what type of espresso maker you choose, there are a few simple steps to follow to ensure the success of your brew. The Italians, who are espresso experts, have several traditional rules that are key to producing the ultimate coffee experience: a perfect cup of espresso. These are the four M's, which are carried out conscientiously by the barista, the espresso bartender.

"Barista" is an honorable employment title that is earned through proven skill and experience, fusing art and science. Many of us may never achieve this professional status; however, the following four Italian guidelines may help us to create a more perfect espresso.

La Macchina (pronounced "ma-keen-a"): The Machine

- The home-based barista may use a smaller version of the more expensive restaurant-style espresso machine; however, the machine must be able to heat the water to 194°F (90°C) and also be able to exert a pressure of at least 9 atmospheres.
- At all times, the espresso machine must be operating efficiently and its utensils kept clean.
- The economical moka pot will produce a strong espresso; however, the brew will usually lack the rich creamy intensity of machine-made espressos, due to the lack

of sufficient pressure. (The stovetop method, however, does produce a perfect coffee for caffe lattes.)

La Micsela (pronounced "mis-shay-la"): The Coffee Blend

- The coffee beans selected, roasted, and blended should provide a harmonious balance between bitterness and acidity, producing a rich, full body, with a fragrant aroma, as well as possessing a thick caramel-like texture. Espresso blends are usually 100 percent arabica, from various origins.
- Personally, I prefer a coffee bean blend of 80 percent arabica and 20 percent robusta. The arabica proportion provides rich, round, smooth coffee body and the robusta proportion produces strength and intensity, responsible for the lingering, almost nutty, aftertaste.
- Ultimately, the espresso blend each person considers the best is a matter of personal taste.

La Macinatura (pronounced "ma-chee-na-too-ra"): The Grinding

- To achieve the freshest flavor from the coffee beans, one should always grind them just before use, because a fine grind increases the coffee's surface area, thereby allowing oxygen and light to steal the beans' precious aromas!
- A burr-type grinder is ideal, since the coffee grind can be adjusted to suit each model of espresso machine. The ideal extraction time (the length of time the hot water is in contact with the ground coffee) for home-brewing methods is 15 to 20 seconds.
- Since the brewing time for espresso is so short, the ground coffee should be fine and powdery, so that the hot water can steep through it at a consistent and uniform pace. The extraction rate should be quick and thorough.

La Mano (pronounced "mah-no"): Hand Making the Espresso

- The hand of the espresso operator and his or her skill ensure that the previous three rules are followed.
- The hand is also responsible for dispensing the correct amount of coffee, known as the "dose." Ideally, a dose is $^1/_4$ to $^1/_2$ ounce (7 to 12 g) of coffee per 1 to $1^1/_2$ ounces (30 to 42 ml) of fresh water. These amounts may vary, depending on the fineness of the coffee grind and its blend.
- The hand performs "the tamping" (pressing down) of the ground coffee in the filter of the machine. The coffee must be evenly and firmly distributed, to allow the water filtering through to produce a consistent extraction.

Tamping

Tamping is a necessary step before brewing in all but the stovetop moka method because the water in the espresso-making device will be under pressure from the machine at 8 to 10 times the weight of gravity and will naturally find the path of least resistance through the coffee. If the water encounters loose channels in the ground coffee, it will rush through these areas, taking the easy way out, which will overextract the coffee surrounding the channels and underextract the coffee between the channels. The resulting espresso will be bitter and astringent.

TAMPING TIPS

- Press the ground coffee down firmly and uniformly in the filter.
- The tamper (the tool used to press down the espresso in the filter) should be applied to the coffee straight and head-on. If it's pressed at an angle, the level of the coffee will be inconsistent.
- Tamp the coffee four times in a "north, south, east, and west" format on the

inside diameter of the filter basket. This will evenly compact the coffee, giving the water a uniform bed to brew through.

- Packed down too lightly, the brewed espresso will be watered down, lacking flavor and body, and may taste burnt from being overextracted.
- When the espresso is evenly packed down into a smooth and polished surface, then the filter can be mounted into the espresso machine to begin brewing.
- The final assessment to the quality control of your tamping is the wet, spent grounds, which determine the quality of coffee extraction. If "worm holes" are present in the wet coffee pack, then the water has found weak spots to channel through.
- When the wet, spent grounds are knocked out of the filter, they should come out cleanly in the form of a small hockey puck. If the grounds fall out in the form of crumbly mush, then the grind and/or the tamp were not correct.
- Essentially, it takes practice, and more practice, to pack grounds perfectly.

Chapter 4

Making Coffee Drinks

*The thick, foaming milk isn't just poured into cups of
waiting espresso, it's dolloped and swooshed and scooped
with spoons and spatulas, as a painter uses different brushes.*

—JAN ANGILELLA, "THE ART OF CAPPUCCINO IN BOLOGNA," *TEA AND COFFEE TRADE JOURNAL*

TODAY'S RENAISSANCE and myriad range of creative coffee drink recipes reflect the diversity of our lifestyle. Whatever the coffee drink recipe, cold or hot, alcoholic or not, a garnishing of whipped cream or milky foam can be a perfect perk. Whether you love your coffee white and frothy, cool and creamy, or strong and dark, there is something to be said about milk and cream partnered with the brew. The milk and coffee marriage has been practiced for decades.

Cream of the Cup

In the 1920s, everyone crooned along to the popular love song "You're the Cream in My Coffee." Today, we could probably sing along to "You're the Topping on My No-Foam Double-Soy Decaf Latte." In the rapidly growing specialty beverage niche, coffee is not the only hot seller. Milk, in both new and traditional forms, is also being consumed as a specialty drink. In fact, my daughter Krista loves milk steamers.

The dairy component is essential to the completion of such modern coffee creations as frothy cappuccinos and tall, steamy lattes, which are made from a variety of all milk types, ranging from creams down the milk fat scale to 1 percent and skim milk. (Some espresso beverage drinkers prefer lactose-free milk, or soy, rice, or other nondairy milk equivalents, for personal or health reasons.) There are many schools of thought on the type of milk to use for the best frothing results. I know a restaurant owner who prepared her patrons' cappuccinos and lattes with half-and-half because it tasted richer.

These milk variations have generated a newfound espresso vocabulary that is based on the fat content, quantity, and style of milk served in the beverages: "skinny," "tall," "grande," "twiggy," "dry," "wet," and so on. Then there are the elusive descriptions of those milks: "frothing," "steaming," "foaming," whatever! It is easy to become frustrated by all of these new terms. The straight talk on this java-jive is that, with enough patience and finesse, the art of steaming and frothing milk can be fun to learn in the comfort of your own kitchen. First, however, we need a clear understanding of some of the basic differences within the dairy jargon:

Steamed Milk

Steamed milk has been heated or scalded to just below the boiling point by the injection of steam or by a heat source. Aeration (or the incorporation of hot air) of the milk is minimal, so the milk's volume is unchanged, and there is only a small amount of froth (microbubbles).

Frothed Milk

Frothed (foamed) milk has been both heated and aerated, by injecting a wand of hot steam at the surface of the milk. This creates a microfoam of tiny air bubbles, giving the milk an ideal consistency of very light whipped cream.

Classic Cappuccino

Typically, cappuccino is made with espresso combined with two kinds of heated milk, steamed and frothed. The classic recipe is one-third espresso, one-third steamed milk, and one-third frothed milk.

Caffè Latte

This Italian family breakfast drink is made with one part espresso to two or three parts steamed milk. The milk is not frothed. (The French call this drink *café au lait*, but they generally add more milk and like to serve it in bowls.) This is a favorite of my cousin, Chef Karl Ludwig, the third-generation chef at my grandmother's Bavarian restaurant.

How to Steam and Froth Milk

TIPS: MILK

Any liquid can be steamed, but achieving frothy nirvana from milk is dependent on the protein and fat that it contains. Fat provides the flavor and "mouthfeel," which is why in Italy they usually use whole milk. Whichever type of milk you prefer to use is the right one for you.

- Skim milk produces foam fastest, but with dry (no fun) stiff peaks called "dry foam."
- 1% milk produces basic, good results.
- 2% milk contains enough milk fat to enhance the flavor of the beverage and is the best, standard midrange milk for the espresso beverages offered in hotels and restaurants.

Most Important: When steaming or frothing milk, everything should start out ice cold; just as in brewing espresso everything should be hot.

TIPS: TOOLS

There are a few budget or so-called alternate frothing methods for frothing milk, ranging from a French-press coffee apparatus (see page 40) to the aeration of milk in a saucepan

> **Cleaning Tip**
> A simple trick I always use and recommend for cleaning the steam wand is to soak it in hot, heavily salted water rather than traditionally suggested vinegared water. Hot salt water breaks down the hardened calcified milk deposits that often plug up the steam wand and also lead to mechanical problems if the milk buildup increases.

on the stove with a flexible, loosewired whisk (see page 77). For standard steaming/frothing methods, the following tools are recommended:

- A 2-cup (500 ml) stainless-steel container or frothing pitcher.
- A cooking thermometer (needle or digital) that reads up to 220°F (104°C).
- Optional milk frothing gadgets, such as a stovetop steamer or a "steam toy," which can produce great foam and steamed milk.
- If you wish to pour latte art (see page 85), you need to have a great steaming jug/pitcher with a pour spout on the lip of the jug.

TIPS: PREPARATION

- Before beginning, make sure all the equipment to be used has been cleaned and rinsed thoroughly, since, as we all know, hot milk can breed bacteria. (This has always been a pet peeve with me.)
- Before using any manufacturer's home espresso machine, please read its enclosed instructions carefully.
- Make sure the milk and the frothing pitcher are very cold.
- Always prepare the milk just before brewing the espresso, to ensure that the final

beverage will be enjoyed at its hottest. (Heated milk can withstand waiting a minute or two better than espresso can.)

🌰 If you are using an espresso machine, blow out any leftover condensed water or clogged milk solids by opening the steam valve into an empty container, then shut it off.

How to Froth Milk Using a Steam Wand

This frothing technique uses 6 to 7 ounces (170 to 190 ml) of milk to make two cappuccinos.

Fill the stainless-steel frothing pitcher one-third full of milk for frothing.

Insert a cooking thermometer into the pitcher (you could also use the clip-on variety).

Hold the pitcher by its handle; place it under the steam wand or jet.

Position the tip of the steam wand just beneath the surface of the milk.

Open the steam valve fully.

If the surface of the milk becomes violently turbulent, and big bubbles form, then move the nozzle deeper into the liquid and turn down the steam a little.

Look for small, even bubbles. The goal is to aerate the milk to a satiny velvety texture.

The sounds you hear will be your navigation guide to correct frothing:

🌰 Wrong-way sound: If it sounds as if you are blowing bubbles through a straw, then it is incorrect. This bubble-bath-like foam will quickly deflate. The sound signals that the steam wand is not positioned deeply enough in the milk and that you do not have enough steam pressure.

🌰 Right-way sound: A deep-down serious rumbling sound is correct. The milk should also be increasing in volume.

Froth the milk until it has doubled in volume (the pitcher should be hot to the touch).

Turn off the steam when the temperature hits 140°F (60°C). The temperature will continue to rise after you remove the wand from the milk. The maximum temperature should be 160°F (71°C). (Frothed milk will be a few degrees cooler than steamed milk, since it incorporates air.)

Wipe the nozzle thoroughly with a hot, clean, damp cloth. With your hands safely clear, turn the steam valve on to flush and clear out any milk in the wand.

Never refroth the milk, ever! It contains too much condensed water for good results.

Never bring the milk to over 160°F (71°C). It will boil the milk, which will not be as sweet and may even have a burnt flavor.

How to Steam Milk Using a Steam Wand

This steaming technique heats the milk without frothing it.

Fill the stainless-steel pitcher two-thirds full of milk for steaming. (There are two schools of thought regarding temperature: Most coffee enthusiasts prefer to begin with ice-cold milk refrigerated in the pitcher. Others prefer using milk at room temperature. Either way works and is a personal preference.)

Insert a cooking thermometer into the pitcher (you could also use the clip-on variety).

Holding the pitcher by its handle, place it under the steam wand or jet. Always make sure the machine is full of steam before you place the nozzle in the pitcher.

Begin by burying the steam nozzle deep down, near the bottom of the pitcher, and steam, taking care not to scald the milk.

Raise the steam nozzle and keep it barely immersed at the top edge of the milk. As the foam begins to build, move the nozzle upward with the swelling height of the steaming milk.

Turn off the steam wand when the thermometer registers 150° to 170°F (65° to 77°C). (A simple rule to follow is that if the metal pitcher is too hot to hold comfortably for more than a second, then the milk will be too hot and will taste bad.)

Tap or gently bang the metal pitcher on the counter to get rid of the air. What's left will be a thick, creamy milk that looks like whipped cream.

Never resteam the milk.

How to Assemble Basic Espresso-Based Beverages

Classic Cappuccino

APPROXIMATE PROPORTIONS

One-third espresso; one-third steamed milk; one-third frothed (or foamed) milk

1. While hot espresso is being freshly brewed, froth (which steams and foams the milk at the same time) the milk in the frothing pitcher. Set aside for 30 seconds for milk densities to separate. (This is when you see a barista knock the frothing jug on the counter for the purpose of separating the steamed milk from the foamed milk!)

2. Use a large spoon to block the milk foam at first so that initially only hot steamed milk pours out of the frothing pitcher. Pour the steamed milk into a cup or mug—no more than one-third of the cup's capacity. Now spoon the satiny foamed milk on top of the steamed milk, again about one-third of the cup's capacity.

3. Now pour the hot brewed espresso down the middle of both milk sculptures. If you use a clear glass mug or cup, you will see the various colored layers.

Mochaccino

APPROXIMATE PROPORTIONS

One-third espresso; one-third steamed milk; one-third chocolate-flavored frothed milk

1. To make masterful, mouth-watering mochaccinos, I have always preferred to add 2 to 3 ounces (60 to 90 ml) of a prepared rich chocolate syrup to the cold milk prior to frothing it. The thick, creamy chocolate syrup adds a rich texture to the milk and the mixture whips up beautifully with the steam from a steam wand.

2. Once the mocha-frothed milk is added to the waiting espresso, generously crown it with mounds of whipped cream and garnish with chocolate shavings, cocoa powder, cinnamon, and/or a maraschino cherry.

3. If you prefer, you can use plain chocolate milk, following the previous instructions for making cappuccino.

Caffè Latte

APPROXIMATE ITALIAN PROPORTIONS
One part espresso to four parts steamed milk, with no foam on top

1. What is called a caffè latte in America is essentially a monster-size cappuccino in Italy.
2. Steam the milk first and set it aside. Pour the freshly brewed, hot espresso directly into the cup.
3. Pour the preferred proportion of steamed milk over the espresso.
4. Add sugar or a biscotti, if desired.

Caffè Macchiato

1. Steam a small amount of milk.
2. Dot the center of a cup of espresso with just 1 or 2 tablespoons (15 to 30 ml) of the steamed milk, leaving a brown ring of espresso around the edge of the cup.

How to Steam and Froth Milk Without a Machine

There is no need for expensive espresso machines to make frothed milk. A simple whisk can be used to aerate the milk, with a simple stove burner as the heat source. In a few easy steps, you can turn milk into rich, creamy, meringue-like froth to enjoy with your coffee. Soon you'll be coming off like the busy barista at your local coffeehouse, wowing your guests with wonderful cappuccinos.

YOU WILL NEED

- Cold milk, preferably 2% or homogenized. (For quick measurements, fill one of the serving cups halfway with milk and multiply that amount by the number of people being served.)
- A small to medium-size saucepan.
- A flexible, loose-wired whisk.

THE METHOD

PHOTO 1: Pour the cold milk into the saucepan. (The milk should only fill the pan halfway, to allow for expanded foam.) Place the saucepan over medium to medium-high heat.

PHOTO 2: Take your whisk and begin to stir the milk, slowly at first. (Loose, wide bubbles will begin to form. The more you whisk, the smaller and more condensed the foam will become.)

PHOTO 3: Increase the whisk speed as the milk temperature rises. Whisk the milk as if you were beating eggs, and you will notice that its volume will begin to swell.

Do not allow the milk to boil! Boiling the milk will spoil the foam and ruin the taste. If you think the milk is just about to boil, *remove* the saucepan from the heat and continue to whisk away from the heated burner. If you do boil it, you must discard the milk and start over.

PHOTO 4: Continue to whisk and aerate the milk until it develops into a fluffy froth and almost doubles in volume, or you have the desired amount of milk foam. Now you have mounds of steamed and frothed milk to use in the coffee creation you crave, the steamed milk being in the pan beneath the foamy microbubbles on top.

TIPS

- A simple kitchen hand-mixer can also be used for quicker results.
- This innovative technique also allows you to make large quantities if you are entertaining or preparing many drinks at a time.

How to Make Basic Cappuccino or Latte Without a Machine

For I have measured out my life with coffee spoons . . .

—T. S. ELIOT (1888–1961)

Years ago, when I was importing quality Italian coffee beans and machines, I met my customer (now friend) Beat Hegnauer, executive chef for the Banff Centre. He used to tease me about my high-end espresso and cappuccino machines, stating that he knew how to make a basic cappuccino without a machine.

One day, I challenged him and we had our cappuccino face-off. I was so impressed, I decided to share this machine-free cappuccino trick-of-a-technique with you.

This method is a combination of the stovetop method of steaming/frothing milk on page 77, partnered with the stovetop method of making espresso on page 53.

Begin by making your espresso in a stovetop moka-style maker. As this is being brewed on your stove, begin on another stove burner to make steamed/frothed milk in your saucepan.

THE METHOD

PHOTO 1: Once you have whisked your steamed/frothed milk to its desired volume, set the foamy milk ambrosia aside for 30 seconds. The milk will separate, with the steamed milk settling to the bottom half of the pan and the light, airy microbubbles of hot frothed milk floating on top.

PHOTO 2: To assemble the cappuccino, pour the steamed milk into the cup first, then dollop the fluffy frothed milk on top of the steamed milk. Very slowly pour the fresh, hot espresso coffee down the middle (or edge) of the cup through the hot layers of milk.

PHOTO 3: If you choose a clear glass mug, you will see the attractive presentation as the various layers magically separate.

Basic Cappuccino

A finished cappuccino is assembled with:

- One-third steamed milk poured from the saucepan, holding a large spoon in place so no milk foam pours with the steamed milk;

- One-third fluffy milk froth, which is spooned on top of the steamed milk as illustrated in photo 2; plus
- One-third brewed espresso poured from your stovetop moka-style maker.

Basic Latte

A finished latte is assembled with:

- One-half brewed espresso poured from your stovetop moka-style maker; plus
- One-half steamed milk only (not any of the froth) poured into the waiting espresso in your cup.

Stovetop Cappuccino and Caffè Latte Tips

- Before making an espresso-based beverage, make sure the milk used for steaming/frothing is very cold, and the espresso is very hot.
- The moka-pot method is simple, hassle-free, and easy to clean up.
- If you don't have a stovetop moka-style espresso maker, then you can certainly use a regular filter drip coffee machine.
- However, if you are using a filter drip coffee system, be sure to use a stronger, darker-roasted coffee blend. A stronger coffee taste is required to work through the milk elements; otherwise all the milk will drown out a weaker coffee.

How to Make a Cappuccino with an "All-in-One" Machine

The first-of-its-kind Mukka Express, created by Bialetti, is a stovetop cappuccino maker. It allows Italian cappuccino to be prepared in the home, quickly and simply. The Mukka pot combines the traditional stovetop style of an espresso maker with a large pot for holding the milk, and prepares two cups of creamy cappuccino or caffè latte with just a few simple steps.

Fine

THE METHOD

PHOTO 1: Pour filtered water to the indicated fill-line inside the "boiler" bottom section. (Important: The water needs to be accurately measured with the provided measuring cup.)

PHOTO 2: Spoon the accurate amount of ground coffee into the central filter basket.

PHOTO 3: Open the lid of the Mukka Express's top section and fill it to the top with cold milk.

PHOTO 4: Push the pressure button, then place the Mukka pot on the heated stovetop. As the water boils, it works itself up the vertical funnel to the upper chamber and also passes through a pressure valve that aerates and mixes the espresso with the milk to produce the finished cappuccino.

BREWING TIPS

- The Mukka Express's fixed capacity is two (7-ounce [210 ml]) cups.

- This device is for use on gas, electric, and ceramic stovetops only.

ADVANTAGES

- This is an easy-to-use and very simple-to-clean product.
- It is extremely safe and equipped with an inspectable valve.
- It is made of enameled, high-quality, die-cast aluminum.
- In just a few minutes the Mukka Express automatically combines freshly brewed espresso with foamy steamed milk and your cappuccino is ready to pour!

DISADVANTAGES

- This method prepares only two cups of cappuccino at a time. If you need more, you'll need to repeat the method.

"L'Omino" is the official name for the "Little Man" figure symbol on all Bialetti coffeemakers. Over 120 million cups of this authentic Italian espresso are made internationally every day.

When a cup of coffee becomes masterful art, thirst is perfectly optional.

How to Make Basic Latte Art

A *barista*, meaning "coffee bartender" in Italian, is one who has mastered making coffee as a profession. All baristas invest their intention, attention, and passion into the espresso they are preparing. Since the new millennium began, however, this skill has been brewing up a notch to a whole new genre of "latte art." Artisan baristas are now drawing designs atop the foam of lattes and cappuccinos, forming beautiful hearts, rosettes, leaves—even lions, bunnies, and bears! These skillful creators of coffee masterpieces have been dubbed *superbaristas*. In their hands, our humble cup has become an artful experience. It's almost a shame to spoil it with a sip!

In 2000, a group of twelve superbaristas met in Monte Carlo to compare their signature styles and espresso-making craft. This modest competition has since grown to become the World Barista Championship, at which more than thirty-five countries compete annually. Here, the world's best baristas and coffee enthusiasts gather to witness the latest dazzling coffee sensations and to experience the soulful satisfaction of seeing the ultimate professional espresso makers in action. It's like a Superbarista Olympics!

Vancouver-based Sammy Piccolo, owner of Caffè Artigiano, has placed within the top three spots at the World Championships for three consecutive years. In Berne, Switzerland, where the 2006 WBC was held, Klaus Thomsen (Denmark) won first place; Sammy Piccolo (Canada), second; and Matthew Riddle (USA), third. Out of the thirty-seven countries that competed there, it's impressive that two of the top three world barista titles are held by North America. For more information, check out the Web site www.worldbaristachampionship.com.

If your love affair with latte art has already begun (or you wish to give it a try), please enjoy the following section filled with tips and tricks directly from award-winning pro Sammy Piccolo. I invited Sammy to open his heart for you and to share his secrets on creating a heart-shaped design. Have fun, and remember, Sammy says it takes "patience and practice, practice, practice!"

Sammy Piccolo's Heart-Shaped Latte

The espresso is the canvas
The milk is the paintbrush
You are the artist
Final art in a latte cup is the masterpiece

STEP 1: ESPRESSO EXTRACTION (THE CANVAS)

PHOTOS 1 AND 2: Extract 1.5 ounces (45 ml) of espresso using a method and espresso machine that takes 23 to 26 seconds to brew: Fill the machine's portafilter with properly ground coffee and tamp it down firmly and uniformly in the filter. (See pages 68–69).

PHOTO 3: Place the filter in the machine and immediately extract the espresso into an 8-ounce (250 ml) rounded coffee cup. Having a rich crema on top is a key to a better latte art finish. (Sammy Piccolo always uses an espresso machine portafiter that has two pouring spouts.)

PHOTO 1: Purge the air from your steam wand and be sure to wipe the wand clean.

Pour fresh, cold milk into a steaming pitcher until it is half full.

PHOTO 2: Insert the tip of the steam wand near the surface of the milk, to add volume. This is called "stretching" the milk.

Observe for a slight temperature increase in the milk. You will know the temperature has increased by feeling the steaming pitcher with your hand. Then submerge the steam wand farther into the milk.

PHOTO 3: Try to develop a "swirl" in the milk while it's being steamed, by moving the pitcher in a circular fashion around the steam wand. This "swirling" is similar to the motion of whipping cream. The action will make the foam thicker and add texture to the milk.

Turn off the steam wand as soon as the steaming pitcher is too hot to hold with your hand! On a thermometer, the temperature of the steamed milk should be maximum 160°F (70°C).

Note: A steam pitcher with a pointed spout and 8-ounce (250 ml) rounded coffee cups are the easiest to practice with.

STEP 3: THE EMULSION OF ESPRESSO AND MILK
(WHEN THE CANVAS MEETS THE PAINT)

PHOTO 1: Do not allow the milk in the pitcher to separate. The milk is your "paint"—it should look silky and shiny, not bubbly. If the milk in the pitcher separates (or to prevent it from separating), spin the jug in a circular motion until you see the milk is back to one consistency.

PHOTO 2: Pour the milk gently into the middle of the extracted espresso in the cup—being very careful not to disturb the crema on top too much.

PHOTO 3: Allow the espresso to rise by filling the cup with the steamed milk until the cup is about two-thirds full. A "white cloud" should form in the cup.

STEP 4: CREATE THE LATTE "HEART" ART
(THE FINAL MASTERPIECE)

PHOTO 1: Once the cloud appears, lower the milk jug until it is resting on the cup. The cloud should form a circle.

PHOTOS 2 AND 3: Swirl the milk pitcher from side to side by wiggling your wrist to ensure the steamed milk and foam are still completely mixed together. Keep slowly pouring the milk steadily into the center of the cup where the white cloud first appeared. When the cup is almost three-quarters full, gently rock the milk pitcher back and forth to create concentric rings. Finish by gently moving the pitcher so the continuous stream of milk cuts through the center of the circle to the edge of the cup. This creates an indentation at the top and a point at the base of the heart, thus a heart-shaped masterpiece!

TIPS

- Don't lower the pitcher down to the cup until the cup is nearly two-thirds full.
- Pour at a distance, leaving 4 to 5 inches between the cup and pitcher. This prevents too much foam from entering the cup before the latte art forms.
- Try to pour the milk very slowly into the cup. This will give you more time to watch what is happening and become comfortable with the process.
- Remember, pouring a heart is not easy—it requires a lot of love. Good luck and keep practicing!

Method courtesy of Sammy Piccolo, Canadian Barista Champion, www.caffeartigiano.com.

PART II

Recipes

*Enthusiastic espresso and coffee lovers know
Creating coffee drinks is an art . . . and a show!*

*Some prefer straight, strong darker drinks—that's nice;
Latte-lovers like it laced with liqueur, syrup, and spice.*

*For others foamy fancy, flavored whipped cream
Embellish exquisite espresso—a coffee drink dream!*

*Or simply sip an espresso to expand the mind;
Caffeinated to imagine—coffee drinks of any kind!*

Recipes

MANY COFFEE LOVERS, from novice coffee converts to creative professionals like the superbaristas, possess a certain personal passion—and/or addiction—in sipping a cup of coffee. Some extend this insatiable thirst to wanting to learn how to make their own coffee drink creations at home.

There is no specific recipe for living that fits each individual's life; similarly there is no individual coffee recipe to suit every particular taste. However, when one uses one's imagination, there is no end to the number of coffee beverages that are possible.

Today's new coffee recipes are the cutting edge of artistic "Espresso-ism"—a term that refers to the world's rapidly changing coffee beverage culture. New espresso-based coffee drinks are being reinvented constantly, with a frisky aroma of fun and a playful perk. The age of "Espresso-ism" is the era of the coffee movement—wherein a small cup of a dark brew is having a big impact on the variety of beverage recipes.

Making espresso or creating cappuccinos and caffe lattes is similar to cooking. Don't be intimidated, and use recipes as a guide or as a "fun"-damental basis of knowledge. Creatively expand on these and make your own creations. Now, let's keep on perking to try some delicious and different coffee drink recipes. Espresso yourself!

Note: All recipes yield one serving unless otherwise noted.

Chapter 5

Hot Coffee Drinks

No one can understand the truth
until he drinks of coffee's frothy goodness.

—SHEIK ABD AL-KADIR, *IN PRAISE OF COFFEE*, 1587

Millennium Mochaccino

For stellar coffee souls!

1 1/2 ounces (45 g)
unsweetened chocolate

1/4 cup (55 g) sugar

4 ounces (113 ml) hot, fresh
espresso or strong coffee

1/2 teaspoon (1.5 g) ground
cinnamon

3/4 cup (175 ml) water

2 cups (500 ml) milk

Whipped cream, for garnish

2 or 3 cinnamon sticks, for
garnish and stirring

SERVES 2 TO 3

1. Combine the chocolate, sugar, espresso, cinnamon, and water in a medium-size saucepan over low heat.

2. Stir constantly until the chocolate is melted and the mixture is smooth.

3. Increase heat gradually to just boiling. Then decrease the heat to medium and simmer, stirring constantly, for 4 minutes.

4. Stir in the milk, and heat thoroughly over medium heat. (Do not allow to boil.)

5. Whip the mixture with a wire whisk until foamy.

6. Pour into mugs, top with whipped cream, and place a cinnamon stick in each mug.

Black Forest Latte

For a traditional afternoon kaffeeklatsch!

1 ¹/₂ ounces (45 ml) chocolate syrup (page 206), or crème de cacao liqueur

1 ¹/₂ ounces (45 ml) raspberry-flavored syrup or kirsch liqueur

2 ounces (60 ml) hot, fresh espresso or strong coffee

4-6 ounces (113-170 ml) steamed milk

Whipped cream, for garnish

1. Pour the chocolate syrup and the 1¹/₂ ounces (45 ml) raspberry syrup into a 12–ounce (340 ml) latte mug or cup.

2. Add the espresso.

3. Fill the rest of the way with the steamed milk.

4. Stir once around, lifting up the syrups from the bottom of the mug.

5. Top with whipped cream.

Variation: Drizzle the ¹/₂ teaspoon (2 ml) raspberry syrup on top of the whipped cream, and sprinkle with chocolate curls. Place the cherry on top.

Millionaire's Mochaccino

Dark, delightful, and rich.

½ ounce (15 ml) orange-flavored liqueur

½ ounce (15 ml) orange cream liqueur

½ ounce (15 ml) coffee-flavored liqueur

2–4 ounces (60–113 ml) hot, fresh espresso or strong coffee

4 ounces (113 ml) frothed or steamed chocolate milk

Whipped cream, for garnish

Coffee beans, for garnish

1. Mix the three liqueurs in a cappuccino or tempered glass mug.

2. Add the espresso.

3. Spoon the frothed milk on top of the coffee mixture.

4. Garnish with a dollop of whipped cream and sprinkle with a few coffee beans.

Variation: For a nonalcoholic beverage, substitute orange- and coffee-flavored syrups or B-52 syrup for the liqueurs.

Sugar-Free Java Chai Latte

Incredibly easy to make and simply tastes great!

7 ounces (210 ml) milk

³/₄ ounce (20 ml) premium sugar-free chai tea concentrate

2 ounces (60 ml) hot, fresh espresso or strong coffee

1 cinnamon stick

Ground cardamom or nutmeg, for garnish

1. Steam the milk with the steam wand from an espresso machine (or refer to page 77 for how to steam milk in a saucepan).

2. Pour the steamed milk into a large latte mug, and add the chai concentrate and espresso.

3. Stir with the cinnamon stick.

4. Garnish with a sprinkle of ground cardamom or nutmeg.

> **Variation:** Regular premium chai concentrate may be used instead of the sugar-free concentrate.

Recipe courtesy of DaVinci Gourmet Syrups, www.davincigourmet.com.

Italian Delight Espresso

This one will have you so wired, you'll pick up AM radio!

¹/₄-¹/₂ ounce (7-15 ml) amaretto or almond-flavored syrup

2-4 ounces (60-113 ml) hot, fresh espresso or strong coffee

¹/₂-1 ounce (15-30 ml) sambuca (optional)

Whipped cream, for garnish

1. Pour the amaretto into a tempered glass mug.

2. Add the espresso and the sambuca.

3. Top with a dollop of whipped cream.

SALUTE!

Sambucca, grappa, and brandy are popular additions to coffee in Italy: When a shot of liquor or liqueur is poured into a cup of coffee, the Italians call this *caffe corretto*, or "corrected coffee"—which is funny, because Italian coffee rarely needs correction!

Dutch Mocha Mint Latte

A heavenly dessert beverage.

1 ³/₄ ounces (50 ml) chocolate
syrup (page 206)

¹/₂ ounce (15 ml) crème de
menthe syrup or liqueur

¹/₂ ounce (15 ml) crème de cacao
syrup or liqueur

2 ounces (60 ml) hot, fresh
espresso or strong coffee

6 ounces (170 ml) steamed milk

Whipped cream, for garnish

Cocoa powder, for garnish

Shaved semisweet chocolate,
for garnish

1. Pour the three syrups and the espresso into a
   12-ounce (340 ml) latte mug.

2. Fill the rest of the way with steamed milk.

3. Stir once around, lifting up the syrups from the
   bottom of the mug.

4. Top with whipped cream.

5. Sprinkle with cocoa powder and shaved chocolate.

Coffee "Fruit" Cocktail

Isn't a coffee-style fruit cocktail—a "berry" good thing?

2 teaspoons (10 ml) berry jam (preferably a raspberry mixture)

7 ounces (210 ml) hot, fresh espresso or strong coffee

Whipped cream, for garnish

Fresh berries, for garnish

1 ounce (30 ml) fruit or berry syrup(s) or liqueur(s), for garnish

1. Place the jam in an 8-ounce (250 ml) tempered coffee dessert glass.

2. Pour the hot coffee over the jam.

3. Garnish with whipped cream and top with whole berries.

4. Drizzle the fruit syrup(s) over the whipped cream and berries.

5. Serve with a dessert coffee spoon to stir the tasty flavors together.

These three addictive ingredients—raspberries, chocolate, and coffee—have been incorporated into rich desserts for years. This beverage dessert is derived from a traditional Italian dessert recipe.

Turtle Mochaccino

For you turtle lovers!

2 ounces (60 ml) hot, fresh espresso or strong coffee

1 ounce (30 ml) caramel syrup

1 ounce (30 ml) hazelnut-flavored syrup or liqueur

1 ounce (30 ml) chocolate syrup (page 206)

6 ounces (170 ml) steamed milk

1. Combine the espresso and all the syrups in a 12–ounce (340 ml) latte mug or tall tempered glass.

2. Fill the rest of the way with the steamed milk.

3. Stir, and serve immediately.

4. Enjoy and sip slowly (. . . like a turtle).

Crème de Caramel Caffe Latte

Crème de la crème.

2 ounces (60 ml) hot, fresh espresso or strong coffee

1 ounce (30 ml) caramel syrup or amaretto cream liqueur, plus extra for garnish

5-7 ounces (145-200 ml) frothed milk

1. Pour the espresso into a latte or cappuccino mug; add the caramel syrup.

2. Fill the rest of the way with the frothed milk, then spoon some of the remaining milk on top.

3. Drizzle caramel syrup over the foam.

Orange-Kissed Mochaccino

The zest of orange and the richness of mochaccino!

2 cups (500 ml) milk

4 ounces (113 ml) chocolate syrup (page 206)

4 ounces (113 ml) hot, fresh espresso or strong coffee

1-2 oranges, quartered and seeded (grate rinds lightly before slicing the oranges, to obtain grated peel)

A pinch of ground cinnamon, plus extra for garnish

A pinch of grated orange peel, for garnish

SERVES 2

1. Pour the milk, then the syrup, into a frothing jug. Froth with a steam wand until the mixture is well blended into a hot chocolate froth.

2. Pour the espresso into two 12–ounce (340 ml) mugs.

3. Squeeze the juice from the orange wedges into the mugs. Discard the squeezed rinds.

4. Stir a pinch of cinnamon into each mug.

5. Pour the hot chocolate froth into the mugs.

6. Garnish with a dusting of cinnamon, and sprinkle lightly with grated orange peel.

They sit around supping a drink which imitates that in the Stygian lake, black and thick.

—SIR THOMAS HERBERT, DESCRIPTION OF PERSIAN COFFEEHOUSES, 1620

Amaretto Mochaccino

Divinely decadent!

1–2 ounces (30–60 ml) chocolate syrup (page 206)

4–5 ounces (113–145 ml) steamed milk

2 ounces (15 ml) hot, fresh espresso or strong coffee

½ ounce (15 ml) almond-flavored syrup or amaretto

Whipped cream, for garnish

Chocolate sauce, for garnish

1. Pour the chocolate syrup and steamed milk into a 12–ounce (340 ml) cappuccino mug or tempered glass mug, and froth the mixture. (If you prefer to use a frothing jug, then pour into a mug once the frothing is completed.)

2. Slowly add the espresso and almond syrup to the frothed chocolate milk.

3. Top with a dollop of whipped cream, and drizzle with chocolate sauce.

Electric Espresso

Coffee with a shocking "byte"!

$1/2$ ounce (15 ml) dark crème de cacao liqueur

$1/2$ ounce (15 ml) white crème de cacao liqueur

4 ounces (113 ml) hot, fresh espresso or strong coffee

Whipped cream, for garnish

1. Pour the liqueurs into a 6–ounce (170 ml) cappuccino mug.

2. Add the hot espresso.

3. Top with a dollop of whipped cream.

Variation: For a nonalcoholic drink, substitute $1/2$ ounce (15 ml) each of dark and white chocolate syrups for the liqueurs.

Red-Eye Espresso

A nightcap to drift away or stay awake with!

1 ¹/₂ tablespoons (22 ml) chocolate syrup (page 206) or crème de cacao liqueur

1 ¹/₂ tablespoons (22 ml) sambuca

2 ounces (22 ml) hot, fresh espresso or strong coffee

Whipped cream, for garnish

1 maraschino cherry, for garnish

1. Pour the syrup and the sambuca into a mug.

2. Add the espresso.

3. Top with a dollop of whipped cream and the cherry.

4. Serve immediately.

Variation: Omit the sambuca if you prefer a nonalcoholic beverage.

Good communication is as stimulating as black coffee, and just as hard to sleep after.

—ANNE MORROW LINDBERGH (1906–2001)

Brown Cow Cappuccino

A moo-ving beverage experience.

3 ounces (90 ml) steamed milk

3 ounces (90 ml) frothed milk

2 ounces (60 ml) hot, fresh espresso or strong coffee

¹/₂–1 ounce (15–30 ml) B-52 syrup or coffee-flavored liqueur

¹/₂–1 ounce (15–30 ml) white chocolate syrup or white crème de cacao liqueur

1. Pour the steamed milk into your favorite stemmed tall 12-ounce (340 ml) tempered glass mug.

2. Spoon the frothed milk on top of the steamed milk.

3. Pour the hot espresso and the syrups very slowly, on an angle, down the side of the mug.

4. Serve hot. For a proud presentation to your guests or a treat for yourself, be sure to watch as you allow the beverage to settle for a few seconds, to see its layers form!

Oh, fortunate are those whose hearts have often been warmed by this sweet drink!

—GUILLAUME MASSIEU (1665–1722), EX-JESUIT, *CAFFAEUM*, 1738

Toffee Coffee Latte

A coffee-lover's liquid candy.

$1/4$ ounce (7 ml) banana-flavored syrup or liqueur

$1/4$ ounce (7 ml) hazelnut-flavored syrup or liqueur

$1/4$ ounce (7 ml) caramel or English toffee syrup

2 ounces (60 ml) hot, fresh espresso or strong coffee

5–6 ounces (145–170 ml) steamed milk

Ground hazelnuts, for garnish

1. Pour the three flavored syrups into a 12–ounce (340 ml) latte mug.

2. Add the espresso, then the steamed milk.

3. Stir once around, lifting up the syrups from the bottom of the mug.

4. Dust with ground hazelnuts.

Latte alla Orange

Una esperiènza intènsa!

½–1 ounce (15–30 ml) orange-flavored syrup or liqueur

1 whole clove

1 small piece of orange peel

½–1 ounce (15–30 ml) rum

2 ounces (60 ml) hot, fresh espresso or strong coffee

4–6 ounces (113–170 ml) steamed milk

Whipped cream, for garnish

Grated orange peel, for garnish

1. Place the orange-flavored syrup, clove, orange peel, and rum in a small saucepan.

2. Heat gently, just enough to warm the liquids.

3. Remove from the heat and discard the clove.

4. Add the espresso and pour immediately into a tempered glass or cup.

5. Slowly pour the milk into the espresso mixture and stir gently.

6. Top with whipped cream and sprinkle with grated orange peel.

Variation: Omit the rum if you prefer a nonalcoholic beverage.

Banana-Lovers' Latte

Go bananas over this one!

3–4 ounces (90–113 ml) hot, fresh espresso or strong coffee

1 ounce (30 ml) crème de cacao syrup or liqueur

1 ounce (30 ml) crème de banana syrup or liqueur

8 ounces (250 ml) steamed milk

Plain or toasted coconut, for garnish

SERVES 2

1. Mix the espresso and syrups together in two latte mugs.

2. Fill the mugs the rest of the way with the steamed milk.

3. Garnish the top of the drinks with plain or toasted coconut.

4. Serve immediately.

"Rolo"-Way Latte

Let this sweet blend "rolo" you away!

¾ ounce (20 ml) chocolate syrup (page 206), plus extra for garnish

¾ ounce (20 ml) caramel syrup, plus extra for garnish

2 ounces (60 ml) hot, fresh espresso or strong coffee

4 ounces (113 ml) steamed milk

Whipped cream, for garnish

Cocoa powder, for garnish

1. Pour the syrups into a cappuccino mug.

2. Add the hot espresso. Stir only once.

3. Pour the milk on top of the espresso.

4. Top with a dollop of whipped cream.

5. Drizzle the whipped cream with caramel and chocolate syrups.

6. Dust with cocoa powder.

Cappuccino Cream Dream

For an afternoon "escape."

4 ounces (113 ml) milk or light cream

2 ounces (60 ml) hot, fresh espresso or strong coffee

¹/₂ ounce (15 ml) chocolate syrup (page 206) or crème de cacao liqueur

¹/₂ ounce (15 ml) white chocolate syrup or white crème de cacao liqueur

Whipped cream, for garnish

Cocoa powder, for garnish

1. Froth the milk until it is double in volume and frothy.

2. Pour the espresso into a cappuccino mug.

3. Dollop the frothed milk over the espresso in the mug.

4. Pour the syrups into the middle of the foam.

5. Layer the whipped cream on top of the milk, and dust with cocoa powder.

Cognac Mochaccino

Surprisingly light—shamefully rich!

1 ounce (30 ml) cognac

1 teaspoon (3 g) sugar

2 ounces (60 ml) hot, fresh espresso or strong coffee

½ cup (125 ml) prepared hot chocolate

4 ounces (113 ml) milk or light cream

Grated chocolate, for garnish

SERVES 2

1. In a small saucepan, stir together the cognac, sugar, espresso, and hot chocolate.

2. Heat gently over a low flame. Do not allow to boil.

3. Froth the milk until doubled in volume.

4. Pour the espresso mixture into two tempered cognac glasses or latte mugs.

5. Dollop the frothed milk over the espresso.

6. Sprinkle grated chocolate on top.

Variation: The cognac may be replaced with a syrup of choice for a nonalcoholic beverage.

Cognac 'n' Cream Cappuccino

Elegant, yet so easy to make.

4 ounces (113 ml) milk

2 ounces (60 ml) hot, fresh espresso or strong coffee

¹/₂ ounce (15 ml) cognac

¹/₂ ounce (15 ml) orange-flavored syrup or orange cream liqueur

1. Froth the milk until it is doubled in volume, steamed, and foamy.

2. Pour the espresso into a cappuccino mug.

3. Pour in the steamed milk, then dollop the foamed milk over the espresso in the mug.

4. Add the cognac and orange syrup, and stir gently.

5. Serve immediately.

Variation: Irish cream syrup may replace the cognac, for a nonalcoholic recipe.

Sciampagna Latte

Absolutely "sense-sational" sipping!

3 ounces (90 ml) hot, fresh espresso or strong coffee

6 ounces (170 ml) steamed milk

Semisweet cocoa powder, for garnish (see Note)

Ground cinnamon, for garnish (see Note)

1. Pour the espresso into a stemmed champagne glass.

2. Very slowly, direct a stream of steamed milk onto the coffee, to form a heart shape (see pages 86–89).

Note: If a heart doesn't form from the pour, top the drink with a heart-shaped dusting of cocoa powder or cinnamon. The distinctively different presentation in a champagne glass will surely impress everyone!

Recipe design courtesy of Steve Ford, www.eccocaffe.com.

Mint Cappuccino

Watch your guests crowd around this one!

1 ounce (30 ml) crème de cacao syrup or liqueur

1 ounce (30 ml) crème de menthe syrup or liqueur

2–4 ounces (60–113 ml) hot, fresh espresso or strong coffee

Chocolate curls, for garnish

Chocolate-mint candy wafers, for serving

1. Combine the syrups and espresso in a cappuccino mug and stir.

2. Garnish with chocolate curls.

3. Serve immediately, with chocolate-mint wafers on the side.

The Godfather of Coffee

"Da Boss" of coffee beverages!

1 ounce (30 ml) Scotch

1/2 ounce (15 ml) amaretto or almond-flavored syrup

3 ounces (90 ml) hot, fresh espresso or strong coffee

Whipped cream, for garnish

1. Pour the Scotch and amaretto into a warmed coffee mug and stir.

2. Add the coffee.

3. Top with whipped cream.

4. Now, take a "mug shot"!

Café con Leche

A popular Mexican/Spanish way to serve coffee.

²/₃ cup (170 ml) freshly ground coffee

2 cups (250 ml) boiling water

2 cups (250 ml) milk

4 cinnamon sticks

Sugar, to pass around with the coffee

SERVES 4

1. Place the grounds in a French press coffeemaker.

2. Add the boiling water.

3. Allow the coffee to steep for about 5 minutes, or until the grounds settle to the bottom of the press.

4. Press down on the grounds to strain them from the liquid.

5. Place the milk in a heavy medium-size saucepan and add the cinnamon sticks. Bring the milk to a boil, stirring occasionally.

6. Remove the cinnamon sticks with a slotted spoon, and set them aside for serving.

7. Add the coffee to the milk, stir, and divide evenly among four cups.

8. Add a cinnamon stick to each cup and pass around sugar to add according to individual taste.

Vanilla Fudge Latte

Yummy—very much a dessert drink!

¹/₂ ounce (15 ml) white chocolate syrup

¹/₄ ounce (7 ml) chocolate syrup

¹/₄ ounce (7 ml) hazelnut-flavored syrup

1 ¹/₂ ounces (45 ml) hot, fresh espresso or strong coffee

4 ounces (113 ml) steamed milk

Whipped cream, for garnish

Chopped nuts, for garnish

1. Pour the syrups into a warmed mug.

2. Add the espresso and steamed milk, and stir.

3. Top with whipped cream and chopped nuts.

Little China dishes, as hot as they can suffer it, black as soot, and tasting not much unlike it.

—A TRAVELER IN THE EARLY SIXTEENTH CENTURY, DESCRIBING THE COFFEE BEING DRUNK BY TURKS

Recipe courtesy of Lisa Ash and Angela Thompson, Monin Gourmet Flavorings Culinary Team, www.monin.com.

Café Magic

This delightful drink will "deliciously disappear"!

8 ounces (250 ml) hot, fresh espresso or strong coffee

¹/₂ ounce (15 ml) Irish cream liqueur

¹/₂ ounce (15 ml) amaretto

¹/₂ ounce (15 ml) coffee-flavored liqueur

Whipped cream, for garnish

2–4 chocolate-covered coffee beans, for garnish

1. Pour the hot coffee into a 10- to 12-ounce (310 to 340 ml) footed coffee mug.

2. Add all the liqueurs and stir gently.

3. Garnish with whipped cream and chocolate-covered coffee beans.

So when the angel of the darker drink
At last shall find you by the river brink
And, offering his Cup, invite your Soul
Forth to your lips to quaff—you shall not shrink.

—EDWARD FITZGERALD (1809–1883), *THE RUBÁIYÁT OF OMAR KHAYYÁM*

Recipe courtesy of P. F. Chang's China Bistro, www.pfchangs.com.

SAMMY PICCOLO, 2006 Canadian Barista Champion, is "offering his Cup to invite your Soul"—for you to sample his two signature coffee drink recipes. Sammy is a celestial coffee lover. He extends his twin passions for coffee and life to his coffee art masterpieces—creating these recipes to share with the world. Cheers!

Insieme Coffee Drink

This is Sammy Piccolo's signature drink from the 2004 World Barista Championships, in Trieste, Italy. Insieme is Italian for "together," which is symbolic of how coffee and the World Barista Championships bring people together.

1 egg yolk

³/₄ ounce (12 g) sugar

1 ounce (15 g) grated bittersweet chocolate

A pinch of curry

4 ounces (113 ml) milk

6 ounces (170 ml) hot, fresh espresso or strong coffee

SERVES 4

1. Whisk together the egg yolk, sugar, chocolate, curry, and milk in a bowl.

2. Pour the mixture into a steaming pitcher, and steam.

3. Divide the espresso evenly among four tempered glasses.

4. Pour the steamed milk over the shots of espresso.

5. Serve immediately.

Recipe courtesy of Sammy Piccolo, Canadian Barista Champion, www.caffeartigiano.com.

Caffè Calabrese

Here is Sammy Piccolo's signature coffee beverage from the 2003 Canadian Barista Championships. This drink is assembled in layers to capture different textures as well as temperatures.

1 ¹/₂ ounces (45 ml) hot, fresh espresso or strong coffee

1 ¹/₂ ounces (45 ml) hot water

¹/₂ ounce (15 ml) orange-infused caramel syrup

2 ounces (60 ml) almond-flavored Chantilly cream

1 Fleur de Cacao dark chocolate disk (see Note)

1. Combine the espresso and water to create a "mini-Americano." Set aside.

2. Pour a layer of orange caramel syrup into a tempered glass.

3. Add a layer of almond Chantilly cream. Do not stir.

4. Place the chocolate disk on top of the Chantilly cream.

5. Pour the mini-Americano on top, to create the final layer.

6. Gently stir a couple of times so the cool cream floats to the top, incorporating all the flavors. Serve.

Note: Fleur de Cacao chocolate disks can be made by double-boiling chocolate and dropping small chocolate circles on a waxed paper–lined baking sheet. These very thin chocolate disks help the espresso "float" on top of the other ingredients (primarily for visual presentation effects). Certainly the chocolate isn't necessary for the final drink, but this is how Sammy Piccolo does it!

> Caffè Calabrese emphasizes the flavors of southern Italy. The ingredients incorporate the nuttiness, smooth creaminess, and chocolate notes as well as hints of citrus that are present in certain espresso blends

Recipe courtesy of Sammy Piccolo, Canadian Barista Champion, www.caffeartigiano.com.

Chapter 6

Iced and Blended Coffee Drinks

*Iced coffee, espresso, and cappuccino drinks
pick up where milkshakes leave off!*

—TOM PEIKO, BEVMARK CONSULTANT

Fake-a-Frappéccino

Oh, "Frappé Days" are here again!

4 ounces (113 ml) cold espresso or strong coffee

2–3 ounces (60–90 ml) chocolate syrup (page 206)

1¹/₂ teaspoons (7 ml) vanilla-flavored syrup

4 ounces (113 ml) milk

3 cups (675 g) crushed ice

Whipped cream, for garnish

Small pieces of chocolate, for garnish

1. Place the espresso, syrups, milk, and crushed ice in a blender, and blend until the mixture is slushy.

2. Pour into a chilled tall 12-ounce (340 ml) glass.

3. Garnish with mounds of whipped cream and small pieces of chocolate.

Money-Saving Tip: Keep day-old coffee cold in the refrigerator ready to freshly recycle into this fast and fantastic frappéccino for family and friends.

Black Forest Iced Mocha

This is formally called, as I know it, my Tante Maria's Eiskaffee!

2–4 ounces (60–113 ml) cold espresso or strong coffee

1 tablespoon (15 ml) chocolate syrup (page 206) or crème de cacao liqueur

1 tablespoon (15 ml) cherry- or raspberry-flavored syrup, or kirsch

2 (2-ounce [56 g]) scoops vanilla or coffee ice cream

Whipped cream, for garnish

Crème de menthe syrup or liqueur, for garnish

Milk chocolate curls or sprinkles, for garnish

1 maraschino cherry, for garnish

1. Pour the espresso into a chilled tall 12–ounce (340 ml) glass or milkshake server.

2. Add the syrups and ice cream.

3. Top with a generous dollop of whipped cream.

4. Drizzle crème de menthe syrup on top of the whipped cream.

5. Garnish with chocolate curls and a cherry.

Coffee-Cocoa Cooler

Tall, rich, dark, and delicious!

2-3 teaspoons (30-45 ml) chocolate syrup (page 206)

4 ounces (113 ml) milk

8 ounces (250 ml) cold espresso or strong coffee

½ teaspoon (2 ml) vanilla extract

8 ice cubes

Whipped cream, for garnish

SERVES 2

1. In a small mixing bowl, mix the chocolate syrup with the milk until the syrup is dissolved.

2. Add the cold espresso and vanilla, and stir.

3. Pour over ice into two chilled stemmed tall 8-ounce (250 ml) glasses.

4. Top with whipped cream.

Iced Café Cola Libre

Sweet, strong, and deliciously different!

4 ounces (120 ml) cold espresso or strong coffee

2 ounces (60 ml) rum

6 ice cubes

16 ounces (500 ml) cola soft drink

SERVES 2

1. Stir together the cold coffee and rum.

2. Fill two chilled glasses with ice cubes.

3. Divide the coffee-rum mixture between the two glasses and top off with the cola.

Java Mojo

A combination of three legendary cocktails and beverages in one—Cuban coffee, Cuba libre, and Mojito!

Lime wedges

2 teaspoons (6 g) sugar

8–10 mint leaves

2 tablespoons (30 ml) lime juice

8 ice cubes

1 ¹/₂ ounces white rum

2 ounces (60 ml) cold espresso or strong coffee

Club soda

1. Moisten the rim of a chilled tall clear glass with a wedge of lime and dip the wet rim into a small flat dish of sugar. Rotate gently to evenly coat the glass rim.

2. Place the fresh mint leaves and lime juice in the sugar left on the dish. Lightly crush the mint leaves with the back of a spoon, and place the entire mint mixture in the prepared glass.

3. Place the ice cubes in the glass and add the white rum and espresso.

4. Fill the rest of the glass with club soda and stir well. Garnish with a lime wedge or sprigs of mint.

Good-for-You Healthy Cappuccino

A nutritious, "no-guilt" cappuccino dessert.

2 (6-ounce [170 ml]) containers
fat-free cappuccino yogurt
(organic, if you prefer)

1 cup (250 ml) fat-free milk
(organic, if you prefer)

2 cups (500 ml) low-fat mocha or
coffee ice cream

Cocoa powder, for garnish

Ground cinnamon, for garnish

SERVES 4

1. Place the yogurt, milk, and ice cream in a
   blender, and blend until smooth.

2. Pour into four chilled glasses.

3. Sprinkle with cocoa or cinnamon.

Variation: Soy or rice milk may be substituted for cow's milk, and soy or rice substitutes may be substituted for dairy ice cream.

Coffee-Flavored Ice Cubes

Don't let your coffee drinks get watered down with plain ice cubes. Making frozen coffee ice cubes is no sweat! Freeze some coffee ahead of time in a regular ice cube tray to use in your favorite recipes for perfect coffees every time.

BREW ANY TYPE of coffee to your personal taste. (I recommend a stronger coffee brew or even espresso for more flavorful ice cubes.) If using freshly brewed coffee, let it cool slightly. Pour fresh brew or even leftover morning coffee or espresso into a clean ice cube tray. Place in the freezer. Once frozen, remove the coffee cubes from the tray and place them in a resealable plastic freezer bag. This keeps your precious coffee cubes from sponging up other freezer moisture/aromas, becoming dehydrated, and shrinking in the freezer. Use coffee ice cubes within two weeks to enhance iced coffee recipes as necessary and desired!

Variations: Cream-Layered Coffee Ice Cubes
For a fancy, fashionable frozen touch, create cream-layered coffee cubes. Fill the squares in a clean ice cube tray half full with coffee and place in the freezer. Once frozen, top the coffee with half-and-half or evaporated milk. When frozen solid, remove from the tray and store in a resealable plastic freezer bag for up to ten days. Proudly serve these fashionable coffee cubes in your favorite drinks.

Liqueur-Laced Coffee Ice Cubes
Add a shot of your favorite coffee liqueur to the espresso or coffee before freezing.

Iced Soya-ccino

A healthy java—good to go!

8 ounces (240 ml) soy milk or beverage

4 coffee ice cubes (page 131)

1. Place the soy milk and coffee ice cubes in a blender.

2. Blend until smooth.

3. Serve and sip immediately.

Note: Any flavor variety of soy milk or beverage is great—vanilla, original, or chocolate.

Variation: For a cool alcoholic after-dinner drink, add 1 tablespoon (15 ml) of your favorite coffee-flavored liqueur.

To give this coffee drink a soy-sophisticated appeal, pour it into a chilled chocolate-rimmed martini glass (see page 170).

"Fast-Slim" Cappuccino Shake

Yes, you can guzzle a shake without the guilt!

1 (11-ounce [325 ml]) can Slim-Fast (any flavor)

2 ounces (60 ml) cold espresso or strong coffee

1. Place the Slim-Fast and espresso in a blender.

2. Blend until smooth and slightly frothy.

3. Pour into a large chilled glass.

Variation: For a hot drink, froth the Slim-Fast first, then add to hot espresso.

Overheard: "May I have a double-tall, half-caf, skinny latte, please?" (Go figure!)

Café Mudslide

Allow your palate to be pleased to perfection!

1 ounce (30 ml) premium tequila-based coffee-flavored liqueur

1 ounce (30 ml) premium vodka

1 ounce (30 ml) Irish cream liqueur

6 ounces (180 ml) vanilla ice cream

Whipped cream, for garnish

Ground chocolate sprinkles, for garnish

1 maraschino cherry, for garnish

1. Blend the alcohol with the ice cream in a blender until creamy.

2. Serve in a chilled pilsner glass.

3. Garnish with whipped cream, ground chocolate sprinkles, and a cherry.

Recipe courtesy of P. F.Chang's China Bistro, www.pfchangs.com.

Espresso "Extreme Shake-Over"

From nervosa to nirvana in just a shake!

3–4 ounces (90–113 ml) cold espresso or strong coffee

1 ounce (30 ml) amaretto or almond-flavored syrup

3 ounces (90 ml) yogurt or yogurt drink

2 cups (450 g) crushed ice

Chocolate whipped cream, for garnish (page 210)

1. Place the espresso, amaretto, yogurt, and crushed ice in a blender, and blend until smooth.

2. Pour into a chilled 16–ounce (500 ml) glass.

3. Top with chocolate whipped cream.

Espresso Ice

So cool it rocks!

¹/₂ cup (125 ml) cold espresso or strong coffee

3 cups (675 g) crushed ice

3 lemon wedges, for garnish

Granulated sugar (optional)

3 rock sugar swizzle sticks (optional)

SERVES 3

1. Blend the espresso and ice in a blender or shaker until smooth.

2. If you wish, rub the rim of each glass with a lemon wedge, then dip the wet glass, rim down, into a small dish of granulated sugar.

3. Pour the drink into three chilled stemmed glasses and serve with the rock sugar swizzle sticks or rimmed with granulated sugar, lemon wedges, and straws.

Cappuccino Smoothie

A creamy coffee meltdown.

2 cups (500 ml) cold espresso or strong coffee

2 cups (500 ml) coffee ice cream or sorbet

1 ¼ cups (300 ml) milk

6 cups (1.3 kg) crushed ice

Whipped cream, for garnish

Ground cinnamon, for garnish

Cocoa powder, for garnish

SERVES 6

1. Place the espresso, ice cream, milk, and ice in a blender, and blend until smooth.

2. Pour into six chilled stemmed coffee or ice-cream glasses.

3. Top with a dollop of whipped cream and sprinkle with cinnamon and cocoa powder.

Variation: For a Mocha Cappuccino Smoothie, substitute chocolate ice cream for the coffee ice cream, and chocolate milk for the regular milk. Garnish with milk chocolate shavings.

Amaretto Coffee Smoothie

An almond—almost addictive—milkshake!

½ ounce (15 ml) amaretto or almond-flavored syrup

½ ounce (15 ml) coffee-flavored liqueur

6 ounces (170 ml) cold espresso or strong coffee

1 ½ (2-ounce [56 g]) scoops chocolate ice cream

Whipped cream, for garnish

Milk chocolate shavings, for garnish

Cappuccino-filled cookie straws (optional)

1. Place the amaretto, coffee liqueur, espresso, and ice cream in a blender, and blend until smooth.

2. Top with whipped cream and chocolate shavings.

3. Serve immediately.

4. For a real treat, serve this with decadent cappuccino-filled cookie straws.

Variation: For a nonalcoholic beverage, use almond-flavored syrup instead of amaretto and omit the coffee liqueur.

Cookies 'n' Cream Frappé

A fantastic frozen frappé for family and friends!

2–4 ounces (60–113 ml) cold espresso or strong coffee

¹/₂ cup (125 ml) milk, plus more as needed

2–3 Oreo cookies or other very dark brown cookies with a white cream filling

1 ¹/₄ cups (280 g) crushed ice

Milk chocolate shavings, for garnish

1. Place the espresso, milk, and cookies in a blender. Add the ice and blend until smooth.

2. Adjust the amount of milk for the desired consistency.

3. Top with chocolate shavings.

4. Serve with fat straws in a chilled tall glass.

Leftover espresso or strong brewed coffee can be stored for a day or two in the refrigerator in a covered container. Use it in any of these refreshing iced cappuccinos. Drink up!

Vietnamese Iced Coffee

This Asian elixir is a classic yin and yang marriage of sweet,
thick milk and intense coffee!

**¹/₃ cup (75 ml) sweetened
condensed milk**

**3 tablespoons (45 ml) medium-
grind French roast coffee**

³/₄ cup (175 ml) boiling water

4 ounces (140 g) crushed ice

Ground cinnamon, for garnish

1. Place the condensed milk in an 8-ounce (250 ml) tempered glass or mug.

2. Place over the mug a cone-shaped coffee filter containing the ground coffee.

3. Pour the boiling water onto the ground coffee and allow the brewed coffee to slowly drip into the milk.

4. Stir up the milk from the bottom of the glass and continue stirring rapidly until well blended.

5. Place the crushed ice in a chilled tall, slender 12-ounce (340 ml) highball glass. Pour the coffee mixture over the ice.

6. Sprinkle with a touch of cinnamon, and serve.

Coffee Break Shake

A chocolate-coffee blend to shake up your daily grind!

²/₃ cup (150 ml) milk

²/₃ cup (150 ml) cold, sweetened espresso or strong coffee

2 (2-ounce [56 g]) scoops coffee ice cream

2 (2-ounce [56 g]) scoops chocolate ice cream

1 ounce (30 ml) coffee-flavored liqueur

1 ounce (30 ml) B-52 syrup or crème de cacao liqueur

Grated semisweet chocolate, for garnish

SERVES 2

1. Blend all the ingredients, except the grated chocolate, in a blender until creamy.

2. Pour into two chilled tall 12-ounce (340 ml) glasses.

3. Garnish with grated chocolate.

4. Sip through fat straws.

Variation: For a nonalcoholic beverage, omit the coffee liqueur.

Espresso Spritzer

Tired of the same old grind? Fizz it up with this one!

1 cup (250 ml) cold espresso or strong coffee

6 ounces (170 g) crushed ice

Carbonated mineral water or soda water

1. Pour the espresso over the crushed ice in a chilled tall glass.

2. Fill the rest of the way with carbonated mineral water.

3. Stir to blend.

Variation: 1-2 ounces (30-60 ml) each of light cream and chocolate syrup (page 206) may be added for sweetness.

Prior to the invention of Coke and Pepsi, it was very fashionable in Italian bars and European cafés to order flavored fizzy beverages made of coffee and sparkling water!

Cola-Coffee

This new and energized coffee hybrid is übercaffeinated!

1 cup (250 ml) cold espresso or strong coffee

4 ounces (113 ml) cola soft drink

4 ice cubes

1 lemon slice, for garnish

1. Mix the coffee and cola together over the ice in a chilled tall 12-ounce (340 ml) glass.

2. Garnish with the lemon slice.

Note: The fusion of these two caffeinated flavors has an espresso-like crema when poured.

Fact: Coffee soda concepts have been around since the 1920s! In 1996, Pepsi produced an experimental coffee soft drink called "Pepsi Kona."

Coffee Champagne

Coffee bubblies anyone?

1 ½ ounces (45 ml) cold espresso or strong coffee

2 ½ ounces (75 ml) coffee-flavored vodka, chilled (see page 166)

A splash of champagne or sparkling white wine

A lemon twist, for garnish

1 coffee bean, for garnish

1. Pour the coffee and vodka into a chilled martini glass.

2. Top off with champagne.

3. Stir the ingredients together gently.

4. Garnish with a lemon twist wrapped around a coffee bean.

Back in the middle of the eighteenth century, Frederick the Great had an uncommon habit of boiling up his own coffee—not with water, but with champagne!

Iced Moroccan

My coffee-loving editor's favorite!

4 ounces (113 ml) cold pressed coffee

2 ounces (60 ml) Moroccan syrup (1 ½ ounces cinnamon-flavored syrup and ½ ounce hazelnut-flavored syrup)

16 ice cubes

4 ounces (113 ml) milk

4 ounces (113 ml) chocolate milk

Ground cinnamon, for garnish

Chocolate sprinkles, for garnish

1. Pour the coffee and syrup into a chilled 16-ounce (500 ml) ice-filled glass.

2. Pour in the milk and chocolate milk.

3. Garnish with cinnamon and chocolate sprinkles.

"Una bella tazza di caffè" is Italian for "a beautiful cup of coffee."

Recipe courtesy of La Prima Tazza, Lawrence, Kansas, www.primatazza.com.

Iced Alexander Mint

A popular and creamy coffee drink!

4 ounces (113 ml) cold pressed coffee

2 ounces (60 ml) crème de cacao syrup

2 ounces (60 g) crushed ice

4 ounces (113 ml) milk

4 ounces (113 ml) chocolate milk

Nutmeg, for garnish

Chocolate sprinkles, for garnish

1. Pour the coffee and crème de cacao syrup into a chilled 16-ounce (500 ml) ice-filled glass.

2. Pour in the milk and chocolate milk.

3. Garnish with nutmeg and chocolate sprinkles.

Where coffee is served, there is grace and splendour and friendship and happiness.

—SHEIKH ABD AL-KADIR, *IN PRAISE OF COFFEE*, 1587

Recipe courtesy of La Prima Tazza, Lawrence, Kansas, www.primatazza.com.

Chocolate Kiss Iced Coffee

Das ist gut—der chocolate kiss!

Simple sugar syrup (page 203), for garnish

Cocoa powder, for garnish

1 ¹/₂ ounces (45 ml) premium vodka

1 ¹/₂ ounces (45 ml) cold espresso or strong coffee

6–8 ice cubes

1 ounce (30 ml) gourmet German chocolate syrup

1. Dip the rim of a chilled swanky martini glass into a small, flat dish of simple sugar syrup, to form a base coat.

2. Then quickly dip the rim into a plate of cocoa, coating the rim evenly.

3. Pour the vodka and coffee over the ice in a cocktail shaker.

4. Shake until the drink is chilled.

5. Strain into the cocoa-rimmed martini glass.

6. Allow to settle.

7. Gently add the syrup and serve.

Recipe courtesy of Stirling Foods, Inc., www.stirling.net.

Chocolate Coffee Fantasy

A decadent after-dinner coffee dessert!

$^1/_4$ ounce (7 ml) vanilla-flavored syrup

$^1/_2$ ounce (15 ml) orange-flavored vodka

1 $^1/_2$ ounces (45 ml) chocolate chip cookie cream liqueur

1 $^1/_2$ ounces (45 ml) cold espresso or strong coffee

6–8 ice cubes

Chocolate shavings, for garnish

1. Shake all the ingredients except the garnish together in a shaker until cold and foamy.

2. Strain into a chilled glass.

3. Top with chocolate shavings.

Recipe courtesy of Lisa Ash and Angela Thompson, Monin Gourmet Flavorings Culinary Team, www.monin.com.

Spiced Cola Coffee

An invigorating innovation for caffeine-cravers!

4 ounces (113 ml) hot, fresh espresso or strong coffee

1 cinnamon stick

3 cardamom seeds

2 whole star anise

1 teaspoon (5 ml) simple sugar syrup (page 203)

3-4 ice cubes

3 ½ ounces (100 ml) cold cola soft drink

1. Pour the coffee into a cup or tempered glass mug.

2. Add the cinnamon stick, cardamom, and star anise.

3. Allow the spices to infuse their flavors together for 4 minutes, before straining out and discarding them.

4. Stir in the simple sugar syrup.

5. Pour the spiced coffee into a cocktail shaker.

6. Add the ice cubes, and shake vigorously to cool the mixture.

7. Pour the chilled coffee into a frosty cold glass.

8. Top it off with the cola.

9. Serve with a straw and chill out!

Iced Orange Mochaccino

Take time to smell this mochaccino!

4–6 ounces (113–170 ml) milk

2–4 coffee ice cubes (page 131)

2 ounces (60 ml) cold espresso or strong coffee

1 teaspoon (5 ml) chocolate syrup (page 206)

2 ounces (60 ml) caramel syrup

2 ounces (60 ml) orange juice

1–2 ounces (30–60 ml) orange-flavored syrup or liqueur

1. Place the milk and coffee ice cubes in a chilled tall glass.

2. Whisk the remaining ingredients in a separate container until well blended.

3. Pour the whisked mixture into the milk.

4. Stir, and enjoy!

Brandy-Mocha Iced Café

Rock your world with this bold, cold one!

12–15 coffee ice cubes (page 131)

1 cup (250 ml) milk

2 (1-ounce [28 g]) squares quality
semisweet chocolate, melted

2 tablespoons (30 ml) brandy or
brandy extract

YIELD: 1 TALL OR 2 SMALL GLASSES

1. Combine the coffee ice cubes with the milk, melted chocolate, and brandy in a blender, and blend until frothy.

2. Serve at once.

The word "mocha" originally referred to a superior quality of coffee beans grown in Arabia and shipped from the port of Mocha, in Yemen. Today, it refers to the delicious combination of chocolate and coffee.

Chapter 7

Coffee and Espresso Martinis, and Coffee Dessert Drinks

The quintessential espresso—now, martini expressed;
Stimulates coffee and desserts with new recipe zest

Straight up, on the rocks, shaken or stirred,
Now—have your coffee in ways that before were unheard!

Espresso Martini

A classic! Sassy and simple!

2–4 ounces (60–113 ml) cold espresso or French-pressed coffee

1–2 ounces (30–60 ml) vanilla-flavored vodka

6–8 ice cubes

A dash of half-and-half

1. Place all the ingredients in a martini shaker.
2. Shake vigorously for 15 seconds.
3. Strain into a chilled martini glass.
4. Serve, and sip slowly!

Cola Coffee Martini

Java cola lately?

1 1/2 ounces (45 ml) premium vodka

1/2 ounce (15 ml) Galliano liqueur

1/4 ounce (7 ml) espresso syrup (page 205)

A splash of cola soft drink

8 ice cubes

1. Shake all the ingredients in a cocktail shaker until the drink is cola-cold.
2. Strain into a chilled martini glass.
3. Serve with a straw and be stimulated!

Mocha Martini

Surrender to a magnificent mocha-moment in time!

¹/₂ ounce (15 ml) chocolate syrup (page 206)

1–2 ounces (30–60 ml) cold espresso or strong coffee

1 ¹/₂ ounces (45 ml) vodka

1 ¹/₂ ounces (45 ml) coffee-flavored liqueur

1 ounce (30 ml) crème de cacao syrup or liqueur

³/₄ cup (170 g) crushed ice

Cocoa powder, for garnish

1. Drizzle the chocolate syrup in the shape of a spiral inside a chilled martini glass.

2. Pour the coffee, vodka, liqueur, and syrup into a cocktail shaker filled with the ice.

3. Shake vigorously.

4. Strain the coffee mixture into the prepared martini glass.

5. The mixture should be somewhat frothy.

6. Garnish with cocoa powder.

Ah, that is a perfume in which I delight: when they roast coffee near my house, I hasten to open the door to take in all the aroma.
—JEAN-JACQUES ROUSSEAU (1712–1778), FRENCH PHILOSOPHER AND WRITER

Tiramisù Martini

The coffee martini you'll want to be fed!

1 ¹/₂ (2-ounce [56 g])
scoops vanilla ice cream

¹/₂ ounce (15 ml) tiramisù-flavored
syrup

1 ounce (30 ml) cold espresso or
strong coffee

²/₃ ounce (20 ml) amaretto or
almond-flavored liqueur

3 ounces (90 ml) whipping cream,
whipped with ¹/₄ teaspoon (1 g)
vanilla sugar (see page 205)

Cocoa powder, for garnish

1. Combine the ice cream, syrup, espresso, and amaretto in a blender, and blend until velvety smooth.

2. Pour into a chilled martini glass.

3. Float the top of the drink with the vanilla sugar–flavored whipped cream.

4. Dust with cocoa powder.

Recipe courtesy of Routin 1883 Syrups/Joseph Trotta/Barista, France Champion of Cocktails, www.routin.com.

Mocha Nut Martini

For the nutty drinker!

2 ounces (60 ml) hazelnut-flavored syrup

1/2 ounce (15 ml) coffee-flavored liqueur

1 ounce (30 ml) tequila

1 1/2 ounces (45 ml) cold espresso or strong coffee

1 1/2 ounces (45 ml) heavy cream

1/2 ounce (15 ml) white crème de cacao liqueur

3/4 cup (170 g) crushed ice

A thin slice of cantaloupe, for garnish

1. Pour 1/2 ounce (15 ml) of the hazelnut syrup, the coffee liqueur, and the tequila very slowly into a chilled martini glass, so that the three ingredients float on top of one another.

2. Combine the espresso, cream, white crème de cacao, ice, and remaining 1 1/2 ounces (45 ml) hazelnut syrup in a cocktail shaker, and shake vigorously.

3. Very slowly pour the espresso mixture into the martini glass, so as not to disturb the bottom layers.

4. Garnish the rim of the glass with the slice of cantaloupe.

5. Serve, and enjoy the new coffee fashion!

Recipe courtesy of Routin 1883 Syrups/Joseph Trotta/Barista, France Champion of Cocktails, www.routin.com.

Amaretto Martini

An elegant liquid dessert!

Sugar, for garnish

Cocoa powder, for garnish

Simple sugar syrup (see page 203), for garnish

³/₄ cup (170 g) crushed ice

³/₄ ounce (20 ml) vanilla-flavored vodka

³/₄ ounce (20 ml) amaretto

¹/₂ ounce (15 ml) espresso syrup (page 205)

¹/₂ ounce (15 ml) half-and-half

1. Mix together the sugar and cocoa powder on a plate.

2. Dip the rim of a chilled martini glass into a separate small, flat dish of simple sugar syrup, to form a base coat.

3. Then quickly dip the rim into the plate of the cocoa mixture, coating well. Now you have an attractive rimmed martini glass.

4. Fill a cocktail shaker with the ice.

5. Add all the remaining ingredients and shake well.

6. Strain into the cocoa-decorated martini glass.

Recipe courtesy of Monin, Inc., www.monin.com.

Coffee Dessert Martini

You can have your drink and dessert at the same time!

2 ounces (60 ml) cold espresso or strong coffee

1 ounce (30 ml) chocolate syrup (page 206) or crème de cacao liqueur

1 ounce (30 ml) raspberry-flavored syrup or liqueur

8 ice cubes

Sweetened whipped cream, for garnish

Cocoa powder, for garnish

Fresh raspberries, for garnish

1. Shake the espresso, syrups, and ice in a martini shaker.

2. Strain into a chilled stylish martini glass.

3. Top with dollops of sweetened whipped cream.

4. Garnish with cocoa powder and a few fresh raspberries.

5. Serve with a spoon!

Cappuccino Martini

For those who prefer tradition to trend.

2 ounces (60 ml) premium prepared iced cappuccino mix

2 ounces (60 ml) milk

1 ¹/₂ ounces (45 ml) vanilla-flavored vodka

¹/₂ martini shaker of ice

Coffee beans, for garnish (optional)

Shaved chocolate, for garnish (optional)

1. Shake the prepared cappuccino, milk, vodka, and ice in a cocktail shaker.

2. Strain into a chilled martini glass, reserving the crema.

3. Layer the crema on top.

4. Garnish with coffee beans or shaved chocolate.

To drink is human, to drink Martiniccinos is divine!

—ANONYMOUS

Recipe courtesy of Oscar Skollsberg, www.stearns-lehman.com.

Creamy Dreamy Coffee Martini

Simply sweet, creamy, and dreamy!

1 ½ ounces (45 ml) cold espresso or strong coffee

1 ½ ounces (45 ml) coffee cream–flavored syrup or Irish cream liqueur

3 ounces (90 ml) coffee-flavored vodka (see page 166)

8 ice cubes

1. Place all the ingredients in a cocktail shaker.

2. Shake vigorously and strain into a chilled large martini glass.

3. Dream on!

Recipe courtesy of Lura Lee, www.ineedcoffee.com.

Irish Coffee Martini

An irresistible Irish infusion!

1 ounce (30 ml) cold espresso or strong coffee

1 ounce (30 ml) Irish cream liqueur

¼ ounce (7 ml) white crème de menthe liqueur

8 ice cubes

Espresso powder, for garnish

1. Place the espresso, Irish cream, crème de menthe, and ice in a cocktail shaker, and shake.

2. Strain into a chilled martini glass.

3. Sprinkle with espresso powder.

One sip of this will bathe drooping spirits in delight beyond the bliss of dreams.

—JOHN MILTON (1608–1674)

Coffee Sands

Smooth and simply sensational!

4 ice cubes

2 ounces (60 ml) cold espresso or strong coffee

1 ounce (30 ml) white crème de cacao syrup or liqueur

1 ounce (30 ml) coffee syrup (page 204) or liqueur

1 ounce (30 ml) coffee cream liqueur or half-and-half

1. Place the ice in a brandy snifter.

2. Pour the espresso over the ice and let it sit for 1 minute.

3. Very slowly, pour the syrups and liqueur one by one into the glass by dribbling off the back of a spoon.

4. Gently mix with a stir stick or cocktail straw.

5. Serve immediately.

Coffee has come into general use as a food in the morning, and after dinner as an exhilarating and tonic drink.

—ANTHELME BRILLAT-SAVARIN (1755–1826), *THE PHYSIOLOGY OF TASTE*

Creamy Orange-Coffee Martini

Memories of hot summers gone by . . . tastes reminiscent of a Creamsicle!

1 ¹/₂ ounces (45 ml) premium vodka

1 ¹/₂ ounces (45 ml) cold espresso or strong coffee

8 ice cubes

1 ounce (30 ml) premium gourmet orange-flavored syrup

1 ounce (30 ml) premium gourmet white chocolate syrup

Curled orange peel, for garnish

1. Pour the vodka and espresso over the ice in a cocktail shaker.

2. Shake until the drink is chilled.

3. Strain into a chilled martini glass.

4. Allow to settle.

5. Gently add both syrups to the chilled drink.

6. Garnish the rim of the glass with curled orange peel.

Recipe courtesy of Stirling Foods, Inc., www.stirling.net.

White Russian Espresso Martini

A classic cocktail evolves into a new coffee fashion!

1 ¹/₂ ounces (45 ml) premium vodka

1 ¹/₂ ounces (45 ml) coffee-flavored liqueur

6 cream-layered coffee ice cubes (see page 131)

1 ¹/₂ ounces (45 ml) cold espresso or strong coffee

3 ounces (90 ml) light cream or half-and-half

1. Mix the vodka and coffee-flavored liqueur in a cocktail shaker with the ice cubes and shake for about 15 seconds.

2. Pour into a chilled martini glass.

3. Pour the cold espresso on top and float the cream to fill the rest of the martini glass.

4. The heavier cream will migrate down through the liquor and mingle with the cream-layered coffee ice cubes.

5. Stir once and serve immediately.

A White Russian is a sweet cocktail made with cream, coffee-flavored liqueur, and vodka traditionally served on the rocks. It earns its "Russian" name from the vodka, but this drink is not known in Russia at all!

Vanilla Espressotini

A caffeinated speedball!

2 ounces (60 ml) cold espresso or strong coffee

1 ounce (30 ml) coffee-flavored liqueur

1 ounce (30 ml) Irish cream liqueur

1 ounce (30 ml) vanilla-flavored vodka

8 ice cubes

Chocolate sprinkles, for garnish

1. Place the espresso, liqueurs, vodka, and ice in a martini shaker.

2. Shake vigorously and strain into a chilled martini glass.

3. Garnish with chocolate sprinkles.

How to Make Coffee-Flavored Vodka:
Soak ¼ cup (50 g) of whole (unflavored) coffee beans in 1 cup (250 ml) of premium vodka for 2 to 3 days. Strain the vodka and discard the beans. The vodka will have taken on the coffee flavor.

Caribbean Coffee Martini

Tongues do the mambo with this Latin libation.

Simple sugar syrup (page 203), for garnish

Sugar, for garnish

1 ¹/₂ ounces (45 ml) dark rum

1 ¹/₂ ounces (45 ml) coffee-flavored liqueur

3–4 ounces (90–113 ml) cold espresso or strong coffee

8 ice cubes

2 ounces (60 ml) half-and-half or coconut milk, for garnish

1. Dip the rim of a chilled martini glass into a small, flat dish of simple sugar syrup.

2. Then quickly dip it into a plate of sugar, coating well.

3. Shake the rum, liqueur, espresso, and ice in a martini shaker.

4. Strain into the sugar-rimmed glass.

5. Top off with a splash of half-and-half.

6. *¡Arriba!*

Frozen "Thai-ramisù" Martini

Flavors flirt in this Asian-inspired dessert drink!

Chocolate syrup (page 206), for garnish

1 ¼ ounces (40 ml) premium coconut-flavored rum

½ ounce (15 ml) Thai coffee-flavored syrup

1 ounce (30 ml) cold espresso or strong coffee

4 ounces (113 ml) vanilla ice cream

1 teaspoon (5 ml) toasted coconut flakes

1. Drizzle the chocolate syrup in the shape of a spiral inside a chilled martini glass.

2. Blend all the other ingredients in a blender until smooth.

3. Pour into the prepared martini glass.

Recipe courtesy of Lisa Ash and Angela Thompson,
Monin Gourmet Flavorings Culinary Team, www.monin.com.

Espresso Raspberry Chocolate Macchiato Martini

A sophisticated sippable with syrups or spirits!

1 ounce (30 ml) raspberry-flavored syrup or raspberry-flavored vodka

¹/₂ ounce (15 ml) chocolate syrup (page 206), or dark crème de cacao liqueur

1 ¹/₂ ounces (45 ml) cold espresso or strong coffee

8 ice cubes

¹/₂ ounce (15 ml) half-and-half or white crème de cacao liqueur

1 chocolate kiss, for garnish (optional)

3 coffee beans, for garnish (optional)

1. Shake the syrups, espresso, and ice in a cocktail shaker.

2. Allow to stand for 5 minutes.

3. Shake vigorously for 5 more seconds.

4. Strain into a martini glass.

5. Top the center of the drink with the half-and-half for a "macchiato" presentation!

6. Garnish with the chocolate kiss or the coffee beans.

Vanilla Cappuccino Martini

Finally, the marvelous martiniccino!

Simple sugar syrup (page 203), for garnish

Semisweet chocolate shavings, for garnish

1 cup (280 g) crushed ice

1 1/2 ounces (45 ml) cold espresso or strong coffee

1/2 ounce (15 ml) vanilla-flavored syrup

1 1/2 ounces (45 ml) premium vodka

1 ounce (30 ml) half-and-half

1. Dip the rim of a martini glass into a small, flat dish of simple sugar syrup.

2. Then dip the rim into a plate of chocolate shavings, coating well. Now you have a chocolate-rimmed glass. Chill.

3. Fill a martini shaker with the ice.

4. Add the espresso, syrup, vodka, and half-and-half to the shaker, and shake vigorously for 15 seconds.

5. Strain into the chilled, chocolate-rimmed martini glass.

6. Garnish with chocolate shavings.

Recipe courtesy of Lisa Ash and Angela Thompson, Monin Gourmet Flavorings Culinary Team, www.monin.com.

Funky Frappétini

The newest jolt in the coffee cocktail circuits!

Chocolate syrup (page 206), for garnish

6 ice cubes

1 ¹/₂ ounces (45 ml) vodka

1 ounce (30 ml) coffee-flavored syrup or liqueur

¹/₂ ounce (15 ml) simple sugar syrup (page 203)

1 ounce (30 ml) whipping cream

1 ¹/₂ ounces (45 ml) cold espresso or strong coffee

Cocoa powder, for garnish

1. Drizzle the chocolate syrup in the shape of a spiral inside a chilled martini glass.

2. Place the ice cubes in a cocktail shaker.

3. Pour the vodka, coffee-flavored syrup, simple sugar syrup, whipping cream, and espresso into the shaker.

4. Give the frappétini a funky shake.

5. Strain into the prepared glass.

6. Garnish with a sprinkling of cocoa powder.

Orient Express Martini

An award-winning coffee drink of Asian fusions.

Ground cinnamon, for garnish

Sugar, for garnish

Simple sugar syrup (page 203), for garnish

1 ounce (30 ml) premium vanilla-flavored vodka

$^1/_2$ oz (15 ml) hazelnut-flavored liqueur

$^1/_2$ oz (15 ml) Irish cream liqueur

$^1/_2$ oz (15 ml) half-and-half

1 oz (30 ml) cold espresso or strong coffee

8 ice cubes

Lemon twist, for garnish

1. In a small plate, combine the cinnamon and the sugar.

2. Dip the rim of a chilled martini glass into a small, flat dish of simple sugar syrup.

3. Then quickly dip the syrup-coated rim into the plate of cinnamon sugar, coating well.

4. Shake the vodka, liqueurs, half-and-half, espresso, and ice in a martini shaker.

5. Strain into the decorated martini glass.

6. Garnish with a lemon twist.

Recipe courtesy of P. F. Chang's China Bistro, www.pfchangs.com.

Zimmer's Frappétini

Intoxicating, addictive, and perfectly legal!

Vanilla-flavored syrup or simple sugar syrup (page 203), for garnish

Crushed chocolate shavings, for garnish

Chocolate syrup (page 206), or crème de cacao liqueur, for garnish

6 ounces (170 ml) Fake-a-Frappéccino (page 125)

Whipped cream, for garnish

1 ounce (30 ml) coffee-flavored syrup or liqueur, for garnish

Milk chocolate shavings, for garnish

Coffee beans, for garnish

1. Dip the rim of a chilled martini glass into a small, flat dish of vanilla-flavored syrup, to form a base.

2. Then dip the glass into a plate of crushed chocolate shavings, to achieve a decorated martini glass.

3. Drizzle the chocolate syrup inside the glass.

continued

4. Pour the Fake-a-Frappéccino mixture into the prepared glass until it is filled to the brim.

5. Top the drink with whipped cream.

6. Drizzle the coffee-flavored syrup randomly over the whipped cream.

7. Sprinkle chocolate shavings on top of the liqueur-laced cream.

8. Stud the crown of this sippable with 2 or 3 coffee beans.

Note: I demonstrated this drink on the Celebrity Kitchen Theater stage at the 2005 Chicago International Housewares Show. Now I'm sharing it with you to enjoy!

Italian Iced Martini

Coffee-lovers will line up for this libation!

³/₄ cup (170 ml) crushed ice

1 ¹/₂ ounces (45 ml) cold espresso or strong coffee

1 ¹/₂ ounces (45 ml) B-52 syrup or coffee-flavored liqueur

1 ¹/₂ ounces (45 ml) coffee-flavored syrup, or coffee-flavored vodka (see page 166)

1 ¹/₂ ounces (45 ml) vanilla-flavored syrup or vanilla-flavored vodka

1. Place all the ingredients in a martini shaker.

2. Shake.

3. Strain into a chilled martini glass.

Recipe courtesy of Lura Lee, www.ineedcoffee.com.

Vanilla Orange Coffee Delight

A tantalizing harmony of taste and texture!

2 ¹/₂ ounces (70 g) sugar

16 ounces (500 ml) hot strong coffee

1 peeled and finely diced orange

2-4 ounces (30-60 ml) orange-flavored liqueur

Juice of 2 oranges

4 (2-ounce [56 g]) scoops vanilla ice cream

Thin slices of orange, for garnish

SERVES 4

1. Dissolve the sugar in the hot coffee and set aside to cool.

2. Divide the diced orange equally among four 8-ounce (250 ml) clear glasses. Pour the orange-flavored liqueur over the orange pieces and marinate for approximately 5 minutes.

3. In the meantime, stir the orange juice into the cooled, sweetened coffee.

4. Add one scoop of ice cream to each glass on top of the marinated orange pieces.

5. Divide the coffee–orange juice mixture among the glasses and garnish with fresh orange slices. Serve with a spoon.

Frozen Frappé Passion

Heat things up with this cold drink!

2 ounces (60 ml) cold espresso or strong coffee

¹/₂ ounce (15 ml) chocolate syrup (page 206), or crème de cacao liqueur

¹/₂ ounce (15 ml) hazelnut-flavored syrup or liqueur

¹/₂ cup (140 g) crushed ice

1 cup (250 ml) whipped cream

Cocoa powder, for garnish

1. Blend the espresso and syrups together in a blender.

2. Add the crushed ice and all but 1 or 2 spoonfuls of the whipped cream.

3. Blend again until thick and fluffy.

4. Top with the reserved whipped cream.

5. Dust with cocoa powder.

Chapter 8

Seasonal and Holiday Coffee Drinks

Christmas cappos to love-potion lattes
Turn festive occasions into coffee holidays!

Cupid Cappuccino

This one is for the young—in years or at heart!

4 ounces (113 ml) hot, fresh espresso or strong coffee

1 ounce (30 ml) chocolate syrup (page 206) or crème de cacao liqueur

1 ounce (30 ml) crème de menthe syrup or liqueur

1 ounce (30 ml) amaretto or almond-flavored syrup

Sugar (optional)

8 ounces (250 ml) frothed milk

Whipped cream, for garnish

SERVES 2

1. Pour the espresso, syrups, and amaretto into two tempered glass mugs. Add sugar to sweeten if desired.

2. Scoop 4 ounces (135 ml) of the frothed milk onto the coffee in each mug.

3. Top with a dollop of whipped cream.

4. Serve with a kiss!

Be Mine Latte

From the coffee cherry of my heart!

1 ounce (60 ml) premium gourmet black cherry syrup

1 ½ ounces (45 ml) hot, fresh espresso or strong coffee

8 ounces (250 ml) steamed milk

Whipped cream, for garnish

1 maraschino cherry, for garnish

1. Mix the syrup, espresso, and milk together in a tempered glass coffee mug.

2. Top with whipped cream and a cherry.

Recipe courtesy of DaVinci Gourmet Syrups, www.davincigourmet.com

French Kiss Caffè Latte

Dedicated to my "French-Swiss" soulmate—Bobbie

½ ounce (15 ml) vanilla-flavored syrup, Irish cream liqueur or coffee-flavored liqueur

½ ounce (15 ml) caramel syrup or orange-flavored liqueur

4 ounces (113 ml) steamed milk

2 ounces (60 ml) hot, fresh espresso or strong coffee

Whipped cream, for garnish

1. Pour the syrups into two stemmed tempered glass mugs.

2. Add the steamed milk, but do not stir.

3. Add the espresso to the milk mixture.

4. Top with a dollop of whipped cream.

5. Serve with a kiss.

SERVES 2

Love Potion Latte No. 9

For the love of lattes!

1 ounce (30 ml) orange-flavored syrup or liqueur

1 ounce (30 ml) hazelnut-flavored syrup or liqueur

4 ounces (113 ml) hot, fresh espresso or strong coffee

8 ounces (250 ml) milk

Cocoa powder, for garnish

Ground cinnamon, for garnish

SERVES 2

1. Pour the syrups into two 12–ounce (340 ml) latte mugs.

2. Pour the hot espresso into the cups.

3. Steam the milk until it has almost doubled in volume.

4. Dollop the frothed milk into the cups.

5. Dust with cocoa or cinnamon and serve immediately.

Irish Elixir Espresso

An old-fashioned coffee cure-all.

2 ounces (60 ml) premium gourmet peppermint-flavored syrup

1 ounce (30 ml) premium gourmet chocolate syrup

1 ¹/₂ ounces (45 ml) hot, fresh espresso or strong coffee

8 ounces (250 ml) steamed milk

1. Pour all the ingredients into an Irish coffee mug.

2. Stir, and enjoy!

Recipe courtesy of DaVinci Gourmet Syrups, www.davincigourmet.com.

Iced Irish Coffee

Lips will stay stuck in the sipping position!

3 ounces (90 ml) B-52 syrup or coffee-flavored liqueur

¹/₂ teaspoon (2 ml) vanilla extract

2 tablespoons (30 g) sugar

6–8 ounces (170–250 ml) cold espresso or strong coffee

A few ice cubes

Whipped cream, for garnish

SERVES 2

1. Stir the syrup, vanilla, and sugar into the cold coffee.

2. Fill two tall glasses with ice cubes and the cold coffee mixture.

3. Top with mounds of whipped cream.

Variation: Coffee ice cubes (page 131) may be substituted for regular ice cubes.

Shamrock Shimmy (Nonskinny) Latte

Lucky leprechauns love this latte!

1 ½ ounces (45 ml) premium gourmet peppermint-flavored syrup

1 ounce (30 ml) premium gourmet cookie dough syrup

½ ounce (15 ml) premium gourmet chocolate syrup

1 ½ ounces (45 ml) hot, fresh espresso or strong coffee

8 ounces (250 ml) steamed milk

1. Mix all the syrups together in an Irish coffee mug.

2. Add the hot coffee to the blended syrups.

3. Pour the steamed milk into the mug.

An Irishman is never drunk as long as he can hold on to a single blade of grass without falling off the face of the earth!

—ANONYMOUS

Recipe courtesy of DaVinci Gourmet Syrups, www.davincigourmet.com.

"Spook-tacular" Seven-Layer Latte

Halloween latte lovers will howl—this is as much fun to drink as it is to make!

10 ounces (310 ml) milk

1 ounce (30 ml) orange-flavored syrup

1 1/2 ounces (45 ml) chocolate syrup (page 206)

1 ounce (30 ml) hazelnut-flavored syrup

2–3 ounces (60–85 ml) hot, fresh espresso or strong coffee

Cocoa powder, for garnish

Black and orange sprinkles, for garnish

1. Steam the milk in a saucepan with a flexible, loose wired whisk or hand-mixer (see page 77), or with a steam wand from an espresso machine.

2. In a cup, mix 3 ounces (85 ml) of the milk with the orange-flavored syrup, to produce orange foam.

3. In a separate cup, mix 3 ounces (85 ml) of the milk with 1 ounce (30 ml) of the chocolate syrup and 1/2 ounce (15 ml) of the hazelnut-flavored syrup, to produce tan-colored foam.

4. Into a clear, tall, tapered tempered 16-ounce (250 ml) glass:

LAYER 1: Pour 1/2 ounce (15 ml) of the chocolate syrup.

LAYER 2: Pour 1/2 ounce (15 ml) of the hazelnut-flavored syrup.

LAYER 3: Very slowly pour or spoon 2 ounces (60 ml) of the untinted milk.

LAYER 4: Very slowly pour or spoon 3 ounces (45 ml) of the orange-colored milk.

LAYER 5: Very slowly pour or spoon 3 ounces (45 ml) of the tan-colored milk.

LAYER 6: Very slowly pour or spoon the remaining 2 ounces (60 ml) untinted milk.

LAYER 7: Very slowly pour the espresso down the center of the entire layered drink. (Important: As you pour in the espresso, keep the drink still so the coffee will create buoyant, separated, colorful layers like magic!)

5. Dust with cocoa powder.

6. Garnish with orange and black sprinkles.

Thanksgiving Orange Latte

You'll be grateful for this yummy drink!

³/₄ ounce (20 ml) orange-flavored syrup or liqueur

¹/₄ ounce (7 ml) amaretto or almond-flavored syrup

2 ounces (60 ml) hot, fresh espresso or strong cofee

6-8 ounces (170-250 ml) steamed half-and-half

Whipped cream, for garnish

Orange sprinkles, for garnish

1. Pour the syrup and amaretto into a 12–ounce (340 ml) latte or cappuccino mug.

2. Add the espresso to the mug.

3. Scoop the steamed half-and-half onto the top of the drink.

4. Top with whipped cream and orange sprinkles.

Pumpkin Cheesecake Latte

A delicious liquid pumpkin dessert.

¹/₂ ounce (15 ml) premium gourmet cheesecake syrup

¹/₂ ounce (15 ml) premium gourmet pumpkin spice syrup

8 ounces (250 ml) milk

1 ¹/₂-3 ounces (45-90 ml) hot, fresh espresso or strong coffee

1. Steam the syrups and milk until hot, frothy, and doubled in volume.

2. Pour into a tempered 12-ounce (340 ml) glass.

3. Pour the hot espresso into the milk mixture.

4. Top with a layer of frothed milk.

Recipe courtesy of R. Torre & Company, www.torani.com.

Happy Holiday Coffee Punch

A yummy crowd-pleaser.

1 cup (250 ml) whipping cream

¼ teaspoon (1.2 g) salt

½ cup (110 g) sugar

¼ teaspoon (1 ml) almond extract

½ teaspoon (2 ml) vanilla extract

1 quart (1 L) cold strong coffee

1 quart (.95 L) vanilla ice cream

1 quart (.95 L) chocolate ice cream

½ teaspoon (1.5 g) grated nutmeg

¼ teaspoon (1.2 g) ground cinnamon

SERVES 35

1. Whip the whipping cream in a bowl, slowly adding the salt, sugar, and almond and vanilla extracts.

2. Pour the chilled coffee into a punch bowl.

3. Add walnut-size chunks of ice cream to the punch bowl.

4. Fold the whipped cream into the punch.

5. Sprinkle with nutmeg and cinnamon.

Orange Yule Delight Latte

"Yule" glow with delight as you serve this!

4 ounces (113 ml) light cream or milk

2 ounces (60 ml) hot, fresh espresso or strong coffee

³/₄ ounce (20 ml) orange-flavored syrup or liqueur

¹/₄ ounce (7 ml) amaretto or almond-flavored syrup

1. Steam the light cream until hot, frothy, and doubled in volume.

2. Pour into a mug.

3. Pour the hot espresso, syrup, and amaretto into the frothy cream and stir gently.

Coffee is the milk of thinkers and chess players.

—ARABIC SAYING, CIRCA 1500

Christmas Cappuccino

Christmas à la crème.

4 ounces (113 ml) eggnog

2 ounces (60 ml) hot, fresh espresso or strong coffee

¹/₂ ounce (15 ml) sambuca (optional)

¹/₂ ounce (15 ml) premium egg yolk liqueur (optional)

Whipped cream, for garnish

Ground cinnamon, for garnish

Grated nutmeg, for garnish

1 cinnamon stick, for stirring

1. Steam the eggnog until it has doubled in volume.

2. Pour the eggnog into a tempered Christmas glass or mug.

3. Gently pour the espresso down the side of the glass into the eggnog.

4. If using the liqueurs, gently pour them into the finished beverage.

5. Scoop a dollop of whipped cream onto the top.

6. Dust with cinnamon and nutmeg.

7. Serve immediately, with the cinnamon stick.

I just had some coffee that was good only for its "sedimental" value!

Snowflake Latte

Mint lovers will melt away with this latte!

¹/₂ ounce (15 ml) premium gourmet vanilla-flavored syrup

¹/₂ ounce (15 ml) premium gourmet peppermint-flavored syrup

1 ¹/₂ ounces (45 ml) hot, fresh espresso or strong coffee

10 ounces (310 ml) steamed milk

1. Combine all the ingredients in a coffee mug, and stir.

2. Enjoy!

Even in the icy depths of winter, retail iced cappuccino and slush drink sales decrease by only 20 percent from their peak selling days during the summer's heat!

Recipe courtesy of DaVinci Gourmet Syrups, www.davincigourmet.com.

Classic Christmas Coffee

A merry coffee to warm the whiskers with!

1 1/2 ounces (45 ml) premium whiskey or rye

2 1/2 teaspoons (8.25 ml) real maple syrup

3/4 cup (176 ml) hot, fresh espresso or strong coffee

1/4 cup (30 ml) whipping cream (unwhipped), for garnish

1 candy cane, for garnish

1. Combine the whiskey and 1 1/2 teaspoons (7 ml) of the maple syrup in a heated mug or cup.

2. Fill the rest of the way with the coffee.

3. In a small bowl, combine the whipping cream with the remaining 1 teaspoon (1.25 ml) maple syrup, and whip until soft peaks form.

4. Spoon the flavored whipped cream on top of the coffee mixture.

5. Top with the candy cane!

Candy Cane Latte

This drink will spread Christmas cheer.

³/₄ ounce (20 ml) cherry-flavored syrup or kirsch

¹/₄ ounce (7 ml) crème de menthe syrup or liqueur

2 ounces (30 ml) hot, fresh espresso or strong coffee

4–6 ounces (113–170 ml) steamed milk

Whipped cream, for garnish

Small candy canes, for garnish

1. Pour the syrups and espresso into a 12–ounce (340 ml) latte mug.

2. Add the steamed milk.

3. Top with whipped cream.

4. Garnish with small candy canes hanging off the rim of the mug.

Midnight Star Coffee Cocktail

A starry coffee spirit to settle back with!

1 ¹/₂ ounces (45 ml) hot, fresh espresso or strong coffee

1 ¹/₂ ounces (45 ml) hazelnut-flavored syrup

1 ¹/₂ ounces (45 ml) vanilla-flavored vodka

4 ounces (125 ml) crushed ice

Whipped cream, for garnish

Cocoa powder, for garnish

1. Place the espresso, syrup, vodka, and ice in a cocktail shaker.

2. Shake vigorously—the hot espresso will melt the ice and dilute all the ingredients rapidly, and the mixture should be nice and frothy.

3. Strain into a chilled glass.

4. Float the whipped cream on top.

5. Garnish with cocoa powder in a "star-dusting" fashion.

Recipe courtesy of Lisa Ash, Monin Gourmet Flavorings Culinary Team, www.monin.com.

Spiced Buttered Rum Latte

A coffee to warm the cockles of anyone's heart!

1 ounce (30 ml) buttered rum–flavored syrup

1 ounce (30 ml) gingerbread-flavored syrup

1 ¹/₂ ounces (45 ml) hot, fresh espresso or strong coffee

9 ounces (280 ml) steamed milk

Whipped cream, for garnish

Ground cinnamon, for garnish

1 cinnamon stick, for garnish

1. Combine both syrups at the bottom of a coffee mug.

2. Stir in the hot espresso.

3. Pour the steamed milk into the coffee mixture.

4. Top with whipped cream and sprinkle with cinnamon.

5. Garnish with a cinnamon stick.

Recipe courtesy of DaVinci Gourmet Syrups,
www.davincigourmet.com.

Merry Mocha Espresso Eggnog

An "egg-citing" holiday coffee drink!

1 ounce (30 ml) chocolate syrup or rum

2 ounces (60 ml) hot, fresh espresso or strong coffee

4-6 ounces (113-170 ml) steamed eggnog

Cocoa powder, for garnish (optional)

Grated nutmeg, for garnish (optional)

1. Combine the chocolate syrup and espresso in a 12-ounce (340 ml) Christmas mug. Stir until blended.

2. Fill the cup the rest of the way with the steamed eggnog.

3. Dust the top with cocoa powder or nutmeg.

Chapter 9

Coffee Syrup and Whipped Cream Recipes and Tips

Coffee drinks dolloped with delightful double cream;
Favorite coffee syrups infused in milk by steam.
Stir in flavored syrups for sipping sensations—
Top with creams for gourmet coffee creations.
Syrups and creams are poured for flavor flair,
Inspired new coffee drinks . . . take the dare!

WHEN ORDINARY COFFEE just won't do, create your own "coffee-teria" and become your own barista! There is a recipe movement out there, and gourmet flavored syrups offer us endless coffee drink experiences with more creative uses for our favorite, delicious flavors. Countless syrup flavors combined with the soft texture of whipping cream can deliver a whole new menu of tantalizing tastes. The syrups provide subtle taste transformations, and flavored whipping creams extend elegant texture and extra smoothness to your coffee drink beverages. For example, a flavored syrup mixed into an espresso base, then topped off with rich, mocha whipped cream, makes for a creamy mocha!

Don't be afraid to explore new flavors. Favorite syrups or any "home café"–made syrups can be added to coffees, espressos, cappuccinos, lattes, shakes, steamers, smoothies, and frappés (don't forget desserts, cola-based beverages, and ice creams, too!). The embellishment of a coffee drink with a delightful dollop of thick whipped cream heightens the coffee-recipe range of possibilities.

The following flavored syrup and whipping cream recipes and tips will help you create extraordinary coffee beverages. Have fun, and remember you only need a hint of syrup to infuse flavor. Too much syrup flavoring will overpower your senses and, as for too much whipping cream—well, it will be yummy but not good for the tummy.

Syrups

Suitable, sensational syrups include: vanilla, hazelnut, mocha, Bavarian chocolate, Irish cream, almond (amaretto), B-52, white chocolate, chocolate mint, caramel cream, gingerbread, tiramisù, and English toffee. Some fruit flavors also work well, such as orange and raspberry. For a wide world of syrup flavor selections, please refer to the syrup companies listed in "Sources and Resources" on page 218.

Flavored Syrup Tips

- When adding flavored syrups to hot coffee beverages, the syrups should be combined with *hot*, not cooled, espresso or coffee, and then stirred. This thoroughly blends the two flavors together. If you are making a milk-based coffee beverage, milk may be added to the syrup-flavored espresso, then stir again. (These syrups taste great on their own over crushed or cubed ice for *cold* drinks, too!)
- Another option for *hot* flavored coffee is to first steam the milk with the chosen syrups and allow it to sit while you separately prepare the hot espresso. The steam infuses the syrup and milk with extra flavor.
- Syrups will eliminate the need for sugar and other sweeteners. Don't add too much syrup, because you want to enjoy the original rich coffee flavor. Remember,

2 teaspoons (10 ml) of syrup are equivalent to about 1 teaspoon (5 ml) of sugar, but will deliver two to three times as much flavor enhancement!

- Spirited syrups: Your favorite liqueur can be made by combining syrup with vodka in a 1:1 ratio: 1 ounce (30 ml) of syrup to 1 ounce (30 ml) of vodka. For example, mix hazelnut-flavored and/or crème de menthe syrup with vodka to make a tasty liqueur to serve with coffees and desserts. Or, mix dark chocolate syrup with vodka, then add steamed milk and espresso for a Mocha Café Mudslide!

- Iced coffee drinks are quick and easy to prepare when using syrups. For each 12–ounce (340 ml) drink, add 1 ounce (30 ml) of your favorite syrup to a glass or cup. Add 1 to 2 ounces (30 to 60 ml) of chilled espresso or strong coffee, then ice cubes; stir well and fill with ice-cold milk. Top with whipped cream, if desired. Garnish with a cherry, chocolate shavings, or cinnamon.

- General measurement guidelines for individual 5- to 6-ounce (145 to 170 ml) cappuccinos, lattes, or cafés au lait: Add 1 to 2 teaspoons (5 to 10 ml) of flavored syrups (or to preferred taste). For an espresso: For every 1^1/$_2$ ounces (45 ml) of espresso, add 1 teaspoon (5 ml) of flavored syrup (or to preferred taste).

- Simple hot café mochas can be made be adding 2 tablespoons (30 ml) of dark (or white) chocolate syrup to a cup of espresso and steamed milk. For an iced café mocha version, simply do the same as for the hot, and serve in a tall glass filled with ice, or, even better—coffee ice cubes (page 131)!

- Smoothies and shakes: By mixing syrups and other ingredients in a blender, you can experience endless summer sipping combinations! A Mocha Café Milkshake, for example, can be made by mixing 2^1/$_2$ cups (625 ml) of vanilla ice cream, 2 ounces (60 ml) of espresso, and 1 ounce (30 ml) of chocolate syrup in a blender.

- Simple sugar syrup (page 203) is recommended when sweetening iced or cold coffee drinks. It dissolves in cold liquids better than does granulated sugar.

Simple Sugar Syrup

Simply the best way to sweeten iced coffee drinks!

Sugar

Water

1. Simmer equal parts sugar and water in a saucepan for about 5 minutes, until the sugar is totally dissolved.

2. Stir constantly. Do not allow to boil.

3. Cool thoroughly and store in a covered jar in the refrigerator. The syrup can be kept refrigerated for up to 1 month.

Note: Many espresso martini, coffee cocktail, iced coffee drink, and dessert recipes call this ingredient "simple syrup." Other common names include "sugar syrup" and "bar syrup."

Coffee Syrup

This versatile syrup is perfect for making iced coffees. It is also great for desserts and over ice cream, too!

2 cups (500 ml) hot, fresh espresso or strong coffee

1 ⅓ cups (350 g) sugar

1 vanilla bean, split lengthwise

⅓ cup (75 ml) dark roast coffee beans, cracked slightly

A pinch of salt

YIELD: ABOUT 1 CUP (250 ML)

1. Combine the espresso, sugar, vanilla bean, coffee beans, and salt in a medium-size saucepan.

2. Cook over low heat, stirring frequently, until the sugar is dissolved.

3. Bring to a boil over medium-high heat and cook, without stirring, for about 4 minutes, or until thick and syrupy.

4. Remove the saucepan from the heat and let cool completely.

5. Strain the espresso mixture through a fine sieve into a small bowl.

6. Discard the coffee beans and, if desired, set the vanilla bean aside for another use (see page 205).

7. Cover the syrup with plastic wrap and chill until ready to use. The syrup can be kept refrigerated for up to 1 month.

Espresso Syrup

Another handy flavoring to have in the kitchen, it is also easy to prepare. This rich syrup can be used as a sweet flavoring in iced coffees (or on waffles, pancakes, or ice cream, too!).

³/₄ cup (165 g) granulated sugar or vanilla sugar (see below)

¹/₄ cup (60 ml) water

4 ounces (113 ml) hot, fresh espresso or strong coffee

YIELD: 1 CUP (250 ML)

1. Combine the sugar and water in a small saucepan, and bring to a boil. Lower the heat and simmer for 5 minutes.

2. Remove from the heat and let cool for 1 minute.

3. Stir in the espresso.

4. Allow the syrup to sit for at least 30 minutes before using.

5. Store the syrup in a sealed jar in the refrigerator. It will keep for several weeks (if you don't tell anyone it's there!).

How to Make Vanilla Sugar:
Wash and dry a vanilla bean, then push it into the middle of a 6-cup (1.5 L) container filled with granulated sugar. Set aside, covered, for 2 weeks. This is now vanilla sugar, with a unique delicate vanilla aroma and flavor. It can now be used for baking (substitute it for all or part of a recipe's measurement of granulated sugar) or for sweetening just about anything.

Chocolate Syrup

Mmmmm . . . very chocolate-y.

1 ¹/₂ cups (330 g) sugar

1 cup (220 g) sifted unsweetened cocoa powder

A pinch of salt

1 cup (250 ml) water

2 teaspoons (10 ml) vanilla extract

YIELD: 2¹/₂ CUPS (625 ML)

Variation: For a spicier version, try stirring in 2 teaspoons (4 g) grated orange peel and 1 teaspoon (2 g) ground cinnamon with the cocoa powder.

1. Combine the sugar, cocoa powder, and salt in a saucepan.

2. Whisk thoroughly.

3. Gradually add the water to the cocoa, stirring (not beating) with the whisk to blend thoroughly.

4. Place over medium heat, stirring frequently with the whisk until the mixture comes to a boil. A layer of foam may form on top of the syrup.

5. Boil for 3 minutes, stirring constantly with the whisk. Reduce the heat if the syrup threatens to boil over.

6. Remove from the heat; pour into a heatproof liquid measuring cup (3 cup/750 ml capacity).

7. Let cool briefly, then chill, uncovered, in the refrigerator until completely cold.

8. Strain through a fine strainer into a 2¹/₂-cup (625 ml) container.

9. Stir in the vanilla.

10. Store, covered, in the refrigerator. The syrup can be kept refrigerated for up to 2 weeks.

Whipped Cream

Whipped Cream Tips

- To achieve the best results and full volume, chill the bowl and beaters in advance. Make sure that the cream (35 percent milk fat) is very cold before it is whipped.

- If using an electric beater, run on medium speed until the cream begins to thicken. Lower the speed and watch carefully.

- "Soft peaks" will begin to form, whether whipping is done by hand-whisking or with a mixing machine at a moderate speed. The "soft peaks" stage is when mounds can be dropped from the whisk or beaters. This is the correct time to add sugar, vanilla sugar, or other flavorings.

- At the "medium peaks" stage, the cream retains the marks of the whip and will hold a soft peak that droops slightly.

- At the "stiff peaks" stage, the cream forms distinct mounds that hold their shape.

- *Do not overbeat.* Like egg whites, cream can be overbeaten. Overbeaten cream begins to look granular, and eventually lumps will form. If the whipping continues, the cream will turn into butter!

- Whipped cream should be used immediately. To keep cream stiff for longer periods of time, add Oetker's Whip It (a stabilizer) or, instead of adding granulated sugar, use confectioners' sugar—it contains about 3 percent cornstarch, which helps stabilize the whipped cream.

- Whipped cream can be prepared up to 4 hours ahead. Cover and chill until ready to use.

- Quick, convenient, and much too easy: Using a whipped cream siphon-dispensing machine is the easiest way to make fluffy, superior whipped cream without the use of a whisk or beater. You simply pour 2 cups (500 ml) or so of 35 percent milk fat cream into the dispensing can, attach a gas cartridge to the dispensing top, shake a few times, and depress the trigger. The advantage to this method is that the unused cream can be safely stored for up to 2 weeks by placing the entire container in the fridge. No bowls, utensils, or countertops have to be cleaned. Simply rinse the container when empty. These fantastic machines are available at most department or kitchen specialty stores.

- Add your favorite flavor to whipped cream or whipped topping by beating 1 to 2 tablespoons (15 to 30 ml) of your favorite syrup into 2 cups (500 ml) of whipping cream. Beat until medium or stiff peaks form. Some suggested flavors are: B-52, almond (amaretto), caramel cream, mocha, and English toffee.

Vanilla Whipped Cream

This one's a keeper! Here is a traditional European recipe I learned from Tante Maria.

2 cups (500 ml) chilled whipping cream (35 percent milk fat)

3 tablespoons (43 g) vanilla sugar (see page 205), or purchase commercially prepared

YIELD: ABOUT 3 CUPS (750 ML)

1. Whip the cream with an electric mixer on medium speed until soft peaks form.

2. Add the vanilla sugar, 1 tablespoon (14 g) at a time.

3. Do not overbeat.

4. Serve immediately or store in the refrigerator for up to 4 hours before serving.

Espresso Whipped Cream

An over-the-top überespresso indulgence!

1 cup (250 ml) chilled whipping cream

3 tablespoons (43 g) light brown sugar

1 teaspoon (5 ml) vanilla extract

1 teaspoon (3 g) instant espresso powder

YIELD: ABOUT 2 CUPS (500 ML)

1. Whip all the ingredients in a medium-size, chilled bowl until soft peaks form.

2. Serve immediately, or store in the refrigerator until needed.

Coffee Liqueur Whipped Cream

Absolutely fabulous on any coffee cocktail!

1 cup (250 ml) chilled whipping cream

½ cup (110 g) sifted confectioners' sugar

3 tablespoons (45 ml) coffee syrup (page 204) or coffee-flavored liqueur

YIELD: 2 CUPS (500 ML)

1. Whip the whipping cream in a chilled mixing bowl until foamy.

2. Gradually add the sugar.

3. Whip until soft peaks form.

4. Fold in the syrup.

5. Cover and chill until ready to serve.

Chocolate Whipped Cream

A chocolate-lover's topping for mochaccinos, or for a plain cup of joe.

1 cup (250 ml) chilled whipping cream

3 tablespoons (43 g) confectioners' sugar

2 tablespoons (28 g) semisweet cocoa powder

¹/₂ teaspoon (2 ml) crème de cacao syrup or liqueur

YIELD: 2 TO 2¹/₂ CUPS
(500 TO 625 ML)

1. Whip the cream in a chilled bowl, using an electric mixer, until soft peaks form.

2. Fold in the dry ingredients 1 tablespoon (15 ml) at a time.

3. Fold in the crème de cacao syrup.

4. Chill for 30 minutes before using.

Coffee Whipped Cream

This is wonderful to use on any coffee cocktail or specialty coffee.

¹/₂ cup (125 ml) chilled whipping cream

2 tablespoons (28 g) sugar

1 tablespoon (14 g) instant coffee

YIELD: ABOUT 1 CUP (250 ML)

1. Whip the cream with the sugar and instant coffee.

2. Chill for at least 3 hours.

3. Whip again until peaks form.

4. Serve immediately.

Cinnamon Whipped Cream

Simply great for all coffee- and cinnamon-lovers!

1 cup (250 ml) chilled whipping cream

3 tablespoons (43 g) confectioners' sugar

1 teaspoon (3 g) ground cinnamon

YIELD: APPROXIMATELY 2 CUPS (500 ML)

1. Combine all the ingredients in a chilled mixing bowl.

2. Whip until soft peaks form.

3. Chill until ready to serve.

Soy Whipped Cream

The alternative whipped cream!

$1/4$ cup (60 ml) soy milk

$1/2$ cup (125 ml) vegetable oil

1 tablespoon (15 ml) real maple syrup

$1/2$ teaspoon (2 ml) vanilla extract

YIELD: ABOUT 1 CUP (250 ML)

1. Place the soy milk and $1/4$ cup (60 ml) of the oil in a blender.

2. Blend at highest speed and slowly drizzle in the remaining $1/4$ cup (60 ml) oil.

3. Blend in the maple syrup and vanilla, adding a little more oil if necessary to thicken.

4. Serve immediately to top coffee beverages or your favorite dessert.

Coffee-o-logy Glossary

From coffee you get upon leaving the table;
a mind full of wisdom, thoughts lucid, nerves stable.

—AUTHOR UNKNOWN, EXCERPTED FROM AN EIGHTEENTH-CENTURY FRENCH POEM

WHEN YOU ENTER a coffee shop or an espresso bar, the wall-to-wall lineup of caffeinated concoctions can be overwhelming. What is the difference between Café au Lait and Caffè Macchiato?

Certain terms and references are used in the language of coffee to describe various bean types, coffee-making techniques, and general barista procedures. The following glossary will enable coffee-loving enthusiasts to achieve a basic understanding of espresso-based coffee beverages. It may also help you look like a coffee pro when ordering!

AMERICANO: This refers to a 6-ounce (170 ml) serving of espresso diluted with water.

ARABICA: A specific variety of coffee. One of the two main coffee species, arabica beans are considered to be the best variety of coffee. It is still the most widely grown. Arabica beans produce the best flavors because they are grown mainly at high altitudes in semitropical climates near the equator. They naturally contain about 1.1 percent caffeine; robusta beans have about 2.2 percent caffeine, double that of the arabica.

BARISTA: In Italian, *barista* means "coffee bartender." A barista is a person who is a master of the espresso machine and makes coffee as a profession.

BLEND: A mixture of two or more varieties of coffee beans from different parts of the world, and sometimes from different roasts. A roaster usually has secret recipes with which to produce customized house blends.

BREVE: Made with steamed half-and-half instead of milk, such as a breve latte, a breve mocha, or a breve cappuccino.

CAFÉ AU LAIT: Literally "coffee with milk," a French version of the Italian CAFFÈ LATTE, this is a popular French breakfast drink comprised of equal amounts of freshly brewed dark roasted coffee and hot or scalded milk.

CAFÉ CON LECHE: In Spanish, literally "coffee with milk." Analogous to the French café au lait or the Italian CAFFÈ LATTE, café con leche is a Spanish coffee beverage consisting of scalded milk and coffee in a 1:1 ratio, often served with cinnamon and sugar.

CAFÉ NOIR: In France, this term or *espresso noir* is used for a single shot of espresso. *Noir* simply means "black."

CAFFÈ CON PANNA: *Con panna* means "with cream" in Italian. This is a straight shot of espresso topped with whipped cream instead of frothed milk.

CAFFÈ LATTE: Its literal definition is "coffee with milk" but, unlike the French and Spanish proportions of similarly named drinks, this popular Italian beverage is one-quarter freshly brewed espresso and three-quarters hot milk. Italians do not add frothed milk, but Americans do. Italians sometimes add more steamed milk than do Americans. Sometimes the drink is really served as a giant-size cappuccino. In English, the beverage is known as "caffe latte," without any accent marks.

CAFFÈ MACCHIATO: See MACCHIATO.

CAFFÈ MOCHA: This is a chocolate variation of the CAFFÈ LATTE. Either cocoa powder or chocolate syrup is added at the beginning of preparing the drink, and the chocolate is mixed (or frothed) with hot milk until thoroughly blended, before the espresso is added.

CAFFEINE: A substance naturally found in coffee that acts as a stimulant. The darker the roast, the less caffeine it contains, because caffeine burns off while the coffee is being roasted.

CAFFEOL: A volatile complex released by the roasting of coffee beans, which produces aroma.

CAPPUCCINO: This classic choice of espresso drinks is made with one-third espresso, one-third steamed milk, and one-third frothed milk.

CAPPUCCINO CHIARO: This is a term used in Italy for a cappuccino that has less coffee and more milk. *Chiaro* means "light."

CAPPUCCINO SCURO: This is a term used in Italy for a cappuccino that has more coffee and less milk. *Scuro* means "dark."

CORTADITO: This is a "cafecito," or Cuban coffee drink, made through an espresso system with a few tablespoons of steamed milk added to it. (In essence, it's a Spanish variation of the Italian "macchiato.") There are many possible recipe variations; for example, sometimes the cortadito is made with steamed evaporated milk and Cuban coffee. Olé!

COWBOY COFFEE: Sometimes referred to as campfire, open-pot, or hobo coffee, ground coffee is steeped in boiling water and then strained to separate the grounds from the brew. Cowboy legend has it that the separation method was often a clean sock, into which the ground coffee was spooned before being immersed in water.

CREMA: A golden-tan foam that appears at the surface of a perfectly brewed cup of espresso. A number of factors are crucial in achieving this: good quality and the correct amount of fresh espresso, the correct degree of pressure, the water temperature dousing the perfect-size coffee grind, and the contact time between the water and the ground coffee. When the coffee oils and colloids are released under pressure and come into contact with oxygen, the characteristic crema is formed on top of the brew.

CUBAN COFFEE/CAFECITO/CAFÉ CUBANO: Essentially this is a "Cuban-style" espresso drink made from Cuban coffee beans. It is traditionally strong and sweet and served in a small cup.

CUPPING: A scientific and ritualized process whereby coffee tasting specialists ultimately judge and evaluate samples of coffee beans considered for world market purchases, keeping notes on specific characteristics of the coffees.

DECAF: A beverage from which the caffeine has been removed by either the SWISS WATER DECAFFEINATION PROCESS, the WATER DECAFFEINATION PROCESS, or the direct contact method.

DOLLOP: This is a term for an unmeasured glob or lump of something soft; for example, whipped cream.

DOSE: The correct amount of espresso dispensed from the grinder to brew one serving.

DRY CAPPUCCINO: This is another version of an espresso macchiato. It is basically an espresso with foam on top, but no steamed milk.

DRY (WASHING) METHOD: This is one of the two methods of preparing the coffee beans after harvesting. The beans are inexpensively—and inefficiently—left in the sun to dry, for up to three weeks. "Dry" beans are less expensive and of lesser quality than the alternative "wet" beans.

ESPRESSO: A dark, rich full-bodied coffee brew that results when finely ground, firmly compressed Italian or dark-roasted coffee is packed in the portafilter of an espresso machine and a small amount of water is forced through the coffee at about 125 pounds (60 kg) of pressure per square inch (2.5 cm), or 9 atmospheres of pressure. The contact time between the water and the ground coffee is very brief, approximately 25 seconds. It is often served in small quantities, referred to as a "shot."

ESPRESSO ALLONGÉ: This is a weak espresso served in France. It is also referred to as *café allongé*. *Allongé* means "lengthened."

ESPRESSO DOPPIO: This is a double 3-ounce (90 ml) shot of espresso, served in a 4-ounce (113 ml) cup or as an ingredient in another beverage. *Doppio* means "double."

ESPRESSO SOLO: This is a single 1^1/$_2$-ounce (45 ml) shot of espresso, served either alone or as an ingredient in another beverage. *Solo*, of course, means "one."

EXTRACTION RATE: This is the brewing time for the amount of soluble solids to pass from coffee beans to brewed coffee, giving it body and flavor. The shorter the brewing time, the finer the grind must be, so that the extraction is quick and thorough. If the brewing time is long, then the grind should be coarse, to avoid overextracting undesirable substances.

FAIR-TRADE COFFEE: Coffee produced by coffee growers, usually subsistence growers, who have been paid a reasonable price for their coffee, based on an economic formula rather than the pittance per pound they usually receive, is said to be fairly traded.

FILTERED COFFEE: This is an economical method of brewing coffee using filter paper to separate the coffee grounds from the soluble coffee. Such a brew is also known as café filtre.

FOAMED MILK: See FROTHED MILK.

FRAPPÉ: This is an iced or frozen drink; a thick cold milkshake. The term is derived from the French verb *frapper,* meaning "to chill." The first-ever frappé was born in Greece in 1956. During a trade exhibition, a drink for children was being promoted, mixing milk, sugar, and cold water in a shaker. Someone added soluble instant coffee to the mix and a cool, refreshing frappé with a special foam was born.

FRENCH PRESS: See PLUNGER POT.

FROTHED MILK: Milk that has been both heated and aerated with hot steam. The ideal consistency of frothed (a.k.a. foamed) milk is thick and frothy, a very lightly whipped texture that holds its shape and can be sculpted. It differs from STEAMED MILK in that frothed milk usually doubles in volume, whereas the volume of steamed milk remains unchanged.

GRANITA: This refreshing frozen dessert is classically Italian. Not as firm as sorbet, it is usually soft enough to eat with a spoon or straw and is customarily served in ice cream cones in Italy.

GREEN COFFEE: Unroasted coffee is called "green."

GRIND: Grinding is the process of pulverizing coffee beans (after they have been roasted) to various sizes to suit the coffee brewing technique being used, and the resulting fineness or coarseness is called a "grind." The actual substance produced is called "grounds."

HARD BEAN: This describes coffee grown at relatively high altitudes, 4,000 to 4,500 feet (1,200 to 1,372 meters). Coffee grown above 4,500 feet (1,372 meters) is referred to as "strictly hard bean." These beans mature more slowly and are harder and denser, making them more desirable.

HARMLESS: This is a term used sometimes by baristas, referring to a coffee beverage that has been made with skim milk and decaf espresso or decaf coffee.

INFUSION: When heated water passes through ground coffee, extracting the soluble coffee, this process is called infusion.

IRISH COFFEE: A classic beverage made of brewed coffee, Irish whiskey, sugar, and heavy cream. It is usually served in a tall glass mug with whipped cream on top.

JAVA: This is a slang name for coffee, dating back to the mid-1800s. Legend has it, this term came from the Indonesian island of Java, which was colonized by the Dutch in the eighteenth century, and became a successful center of coffee production. Java is also a variety of coffee grown in Indonesia.

KAFFEEKLATSCH: This is a popular German term meaning "coffee gossip"—a gathering of people enjoying a cup of coffee along with conversation.

LATTE: Short for CAFFÈ LATTE—espresso with milk.

MACCHIATO: This term literally means "spotted" in Italian. An authentic latte macchiato is a traditional Italian breakfast drink made with one $1^1/_2$-ounce (45 ml) shot of espresso poured into a cup with 8 ounces (240 ml) steamed milk; no froth or foam. Caffè macchiato is simply one serving of espresso with one heaping tablespoon of frothed milk on top.

MEXICAN COFFEE: Coffee brewed with cinnamon and brown sugar, mixed with cocoa, and served hot with whipped cream on top.

MOCHACCINO: Freshly brewed espresso and steamed chocolate milk in equal parts. It is topped with foam from the steamed chocolate milk.

ORGANIC COFFEE: Coffee certified by independent agencies as having been organically grown, processed, stored, and roasted. This means that no synthetic chemical pesticides, fertilizers, cleansers, etc., have come into contact with the coffee trees or beans. Organic coffees cost more than similar nonorganic coffees due to higher costs of production and the additional costs of certification.

PLUNGER POT: This may also be referred to as a "French press," after its original French manufacturer. Ground coffee steeps in hot water in the pot, and then a fine metal screen is pressed down through the liquid to separate the grounds from the brewed coffee. This brew is the next-thickest-textured coffee to professional espresso or what is produced by the espresso stovetop method.

PUMP MACHINE: An espresso brewer that produces high pressure, using a small electric pump. It uses the high pressure to force hot but not boiling water through finely ground espresso. Most quality home espresso machines include a pump.

RED-EYE: This is a cup of brewed coffee with a shot of espresso—double strength!

RISTRETTO: Italian for "restricted," a regular shot of espresso is made with less than the usual amount of hot water, essentially being stopped or pulled "short"; hence sometimes referred to as "short pull." This produces an intense flavor and brings out the espresso's caramel-like sweetness.

ROBUSTA: One of the two main coffee species, robusta is responsible for the strength and intensity of the coffee. It lacks the aroma and smoothness of its competitor, the arabica coffee bean. It grows well at low altitudes, and has twice the amount of caffeine, about 2.2 percent, of the arabica bean, which has about 1.1 percent.

SHADE-GROWN COFFEE: This coffee is literally "made in the shade." It refers to a method of growing coffee in a natural environment that includes shade trees and songbirds. Proponents of this product say that growing coffee in this manner will protect the natural rain forests and protect certain animal species.

SHOT: See SINGLE or ESPRESSO SOLO.

SINGLE: This is basically the same as an ESPRESSO SOLO, a single shot of espresso.

SKINNY: Also called "tall" or "twiggy," this refers to a drink, usually a latte, made with skim or nonfat milk.

SOFT-BEAN COFFEE: Describes coffee grown at relatively low altitudes—under 4,000 feet (1,200 meters). Beans grown at lower altitudes mature more quickly and produce a lighter, more porous coffee bean.

SOYA-CCINO: This is a New Age cappuccino containing soy or rice milk instead of dairy milk. The flavor is slightly different, but for nondairy-imbibing coffee drinkers or those who are lactose intolerant, both substitutes make a good alternative to a traditional cappuccino.

SPECIALTY COFFEE: This can refer to custom whole-bean coffees sold by the countries of origin, or particular roasting styles, sometimes with additional flavors. In general public usage, this term may also refer to fancy coffee drinks; for example, cappuccino or mochaccino.

SPENT GROUNDS: Used (brewed) ground coffee; they are very good for composting.

STEAM WAND: This is the tube attached to home and professional espresso machines. High-pressured steam is delivered out of the end of the wand. It is used mainly to make steamed and frothed milk.

STEAMED MILK: Milk that has been heated by steam. Its volume remains unchanged, unlike that of FROTHED MILK, whose volume is usually double that of the milk.

STEAMER: Also known as STEAMED MILK, this is a coffeehouse beverage that contains no actual coffee. It is heated and "fluffed up" by the injection of steam. Flavored syrups, producing many flavor variations, may be added to the steamed milk.

STRENGTH: In coffee, strength does not refer to flavor. It refers to the ratio of coffee to water. The brew is stronger with more ground coffee to less water.

SWISS WATER DECAFFEINATION PROCESS: A specific method of removing the caffeine from coffee beans. In this process, a charcoal filter, never chemicals, is used to remove the caffeine. Chemicals are sometimes used in the (non-Swiss) WATER DECAFFEINATION PROCESS.

TAMPER: A small tool that is used to press or "tamp down" the surface of the ground coffee in the metal filter holder of an espresso machine. A tamper almost always has a flat bottom, and is slightly narrower than the filter.

THERMAL CARAFE: Best known as a "thermos," this insulated container is the ideal way to store brewed coffee. The flavor of the coffee in a tightly sealed carafe can remain intact for up to an hour. Keeping coffee on a burner for any length of time produces a sour, bitter brew.

WATER DECAFFEINATION PROCESS: In this method of decaffeination, all the caffeine and soluble solids are removed from green coffee beans by soaking them in water. The water process can involve chemicals at certain stages.

WET CAPPUCCINO: A wet cappuccino has more steamed milk and less foam than a regular cappuccino.

WET (WASHING) METHOD: One of the two methods of drying green coffee beans after harvesting to prepare the beans for market. This method is more efficient and more expensive than the alternative DRY (WASHING) METHOD. "Washed" coffees are of higher quality and more expensive than "dry" coffees.

Sources and Resources

I EXPRESS GRATEFUL APPRECIATION to the following companies, manufacturers, restaurants, and coffeehouses that contributed invaluable information and assistance to the creation of this book. For your convenience, I have provided each company's Web address.

Alberta Women Entrepreneurs
www.awebusiness.com

Banff Centre for Performing Arts Executive Chef
www.banffcentre.ca

Bialetti USA
www.bialetti.com

Business Coach and Speaker
www.robinjay.com

Caffè Artigiano—Sammy Piccolo
www.caffeartigiano.com

Coffee Association of Canada
www.coffeeassoc.com

Coffee Kids
www.coffeekids.org

Cook Like a Chef—Clay Frotten
www.kitchens4pros.com

DaVinci Gourmet Syrups
www.davincigourmet.com

Ecco Caffe Coffee Roasters—Steve Ford
www.eccocaffe.com

Hospitality News/CoffeeTalk Magazine—Kerri Goodman Small
www.hospnews.com

Ingrid George/Artist Extraordinaire
www.illustrationsbyingrid.ca

Innovated Products Manufacturing, Inc.
www.innovatedproductsmfg.com

J. M. Glass
www.jmglass.com

Kerry Food and Beverage
www.kerrygroup.com

La Prima Tazza
www.primatazza.com

Monin Syrups
www.monin.com

Nightclub & Bar Magazine
(produced by Oxford Publishing)
www.nightclub.com

Espresso Canada, Inc.
www.espressocanada.ca

Oscar's Syrups
www.stearns-lehman.com

P. F. Chang's China Bistro
www.pfchangs.com

Routin Syrups USA
www.routin.com

Saeco USA and Saeco Canada
www.saeco-usa.com and
www.saeco.ca

Specialty Coffee Association of America
www.scaa.com

Stirling Gourmet Flavors
www.stirling.net

Torani—R.Torre & Company
www.torani.com

World Barista Championship Association
www.worldbaristachampionship.com

Bibliography

Castle, Timothy James. *The Perfect Cup*. Reading, MA: Perseus Books (Addison Wesley), 1991.

Davids, Kenneth. *A Guide to Buying, Brewing and Enjoying*. Singapore: 101 Productions, 1991.

Davids, Kenneth. *Espresso: Ultimate Coffee*. Santa Rosa: Cole Group, 1993.

Dicum, Gregory, and N. Lullinger. *The Coffee Book*. New York: The New Press, 1999.

Illy, Francesco and Ricardo. *The Book of Coffee: A Gourmet's Guide*. Milan: Mondadori, 1989; New York: Abbeville Press, 1992.

Kummer, Corby. *The Joy of Coffee: The Essential Guide to Buying, Brewing and Enjoying*. Shelburne, VT: Chapters Publishing, 1995.

Lacalamita, Tom. *The Ultimate Espresso Machine Cookbook*. New York: Simon and Schuster, 1995.

Lavazza. *Guida al Caffè*. Milan: Centro Luigi Lavazza, 1991.

Roden, Claudia. *Coffee: A Coffee Lover's Companion*. London: Pavilion, 1999.

Rolnick, Harry. *The Complete Book of Coffee*. Hong Kong: Melitta, 1982.

Recipe Index

General Index

acids, 12, 13

Africa, 6–7

almond extract, 189

altitude, 2, 5, 11; quality and, 4

amaretto, 158, 180, 188, 191; liqueur, 102, 156; syrup, 98

Arabian Mocha, 18

aroma, 3, 4, 11, 12, 16; decaffeination and, 27; of espresso, 49, 51; sealing in of, 13

Asia, 6–7

automatic drip brewing method: advantages/disadvantages of, 35; brewing tips, 34–35; grind for, 34

barista, 66, 85

bean(s): arabica, 3, 4, 6, 7, 31, 67; blend, 2, 17–18, 67; botanics, 2, 3; chemical change in, 12; decaffeination processing methods of, 30; espresso, 13, 67; liberica, 3, 5; robusta, 3, 4–5, 6, 7, 31, 67

berry jam, 101

Bialetti, 56, 81, 83

blending: beans, 2, 17–18; beans for espresso, 67

body, of coffee, 3, 4, 13, 14

brandy, 152

brewing: grind and, 22–24; tips for automatic drip method, 34–35; tips for cold-press brewing method, 38; tips for French press method, 40; tips for manual drip method, 36; tips for Middle Eastern brewing method, 44; tips for Neapolitan

filter espresso method, 58; tips for percolator brewing method, 46; tips for piston espresso machines, 62–63; tips for pump espresso machines, 60–61; tips for steam-powered espresso machines, 65; tips for stovetop espresso method, 54; tips for vacuum pot brewing method, 42. *See also* coffee brewing technique; espresso brewing technique

briki, 43

caffè latte, 70, 72; preparation of, 77, 81; without machine, 79–81

caffè latte art, 85; heart-shaped, 86–89

caffè macchiato, preparation of, 77

caffeine, 3, 4, 5, 12; roasting and, 12, 14

caffeol. *See* coffee oils

cappuccino, classic, 59, 70, 71–72; with all-in-one-machine, 81–83; preparation of, 76, 80–81; without machine, 79–81

cardamom, 18, 97, 150

chai tea concentrate, 97

champagne, 144

Chantilly cream, 122

chemical: change in beans, 12; components of espresso, 50

cinnamon, 18, 94, 118, 150, 189

classifications, global, 2

climate, 2, 4, 5, 8

coconut flakes, 168

coffee: body of, 3, 4, 13, 14; camping,

38; carbon dioxide and, 26; commercial, 21; countries producing, 6–7; diseases of, plant, 5, 8; drinking habits, international, 32; fresh water and, 47; freshness guide, 21–22; oxygen and, 22, 26; plant growth, 8–9; seed, 2, 8; specialty, 20; species of, 3, 4–5, 11; strength/intensity of, 3, 5; trade, 6, 11; washed, 10

coffee brewing technique: automatic drip method, 34–35; cold-press, 37–39; French press method, 39–41; manual drip method, 35–37; Middle Eastern, 43–45; percolator, 45–46; vacuum pot, 41–42

coffee oils, 24, 25, 26, 27; espresso and, 51, 59; roasting and, 12, 13

coffee, perfect cup of, 46; clean equipment and, 47; fresh water and, 47; proper quantities and, 48; temperature and, 48

cognac, 114, 115

cola soft drink, 127, 142, 150

cold-press brewing method: advantages/disadvantages of, 38–39; brewing tips for, 38; grind for, 37

countries, coffee-producing, 6–7

crema, of espresso, 51

cultivation, 2, 8–9

cupping, 17

curry, 121